Exploring Music

Eunice Boardman

Beth Landis

Barbara Andress

illustrated by David Chestnutt

HOLT, RINEHART AND WINSTON, INC.
New York, Toronto, London, Sydney

Consultants

Milton Babbitt

Keith E. Baird

Louis W. Ballard

Chou Wen-chung

Dorothy K. Gillett

Alan Lomax

Kurt Miller

Elena Paz

Virginia Stroh Red

Fela Sowande

Kurt Stone

Nelmatilda Woodard

Acknowledgments

Grateful acknowledgment is given to the following authors and publishers:

Atheneum Publishers for "Ping Pong." Copyright © 1970 by Eve Merriam. From *Finding a Poem*. Used by permission.

Belwin-Mills Publishing Corp. for "Praise for Bread." Copyright 1918 by Belwin-Mills Publishing Corp. Copyright renewed 1946. Used by permission.

The Boy Scouts Association of Great Britain for "We're All Together Again" from *The Boy Scout Song Book*. Used by permission.

Venoris Cates for "One, Two, Three." Used by permission.

Cooperative Recreation Service, Inc. for "Walk Together Children" from *Look Away;* "My Head and My Shoulders" from *Third Proof Book;* "Chinese Grace" from *Grace at Table;* "Tambur Andandori" from *Peoples of the Earth;* "Tortilla Vender" from *Amigos Cantando;* "Donkeys and Carrots" from *Rounds;* "I Love the Mountains" and "Derry Ding Ding Dason" from *Sing a Tune;* "Kenya Greeting Song" from *African Songs; and* "Tongo" from *Tayo'y Umawit*. Used by permission.

Walt Disney Music Company for "Siamese Cat Song" (from Walt Disney's "Lady and the Tramp") (Peggy Lee and Sonny Burke). Copyright 1952 by Walt Disney Music Company. Used by permission.

Harcourt, Brace, Jovanovich, Inc. for "This House is Haunted," originally titled "Calliope," from *The American Songbag* by Carl Sandburg. Copyright 1927 by Harcourt, Brace, Jovanovich, Inc. Renewed © 1955 by Carl Sandburg. Used by permission.

Harcourt, Brace & World, Inc. for "Hallowe'en" from *The Little Hill*, copyright 1949 by Harry Behn. Used by permission.

Frederick Harris Music Co. Limited for words as arranged by J. E. Middleton to " 'Twas in the Moon of Wintertime." Used by permission.

Charles Haywood for "The Gazelle" from *Folk Songs of the World*. Used by permission.

Holt, Rinehart and Winston of Canada Limited for "Hallowe'en," music by John Wood; for "Come Boating with Me," words by Lansing Macdowell; from *Songtime 4* by Vera Russel, *et. al.* Copyright © 1963 by Holt, Rinehart and Winston of Canada Limited, Publishers, Toronto. Used by permission.

David McKay Company, Inc. for "Long John," copyright © 1961, © 1969 by Beatrice Landeck, from the book *Echoes of Africa*. Used by permission.

Mills Music Inc. for "The Little Drummer Boy," copyright © 1958 by Mills Music Inc. and International Korwin Corp. Used by permission.

Joseph and Nathan Segal for "Raindrops." Copyright © 1971 by Joseph and Nathan Segal. Used by permission.

Robert D. Sittig for "Valentine, Valentine." Used by permission.

Stormking Music, Inc. for "Tell Us Gentlemen." Used by permission.

Charles E. Tuttle Co., Inc. for "Hitori de Sabishii" from *Folk Songs of Japanese Children* by Donald Berger. Used by permission.

The University of New Mexico Press for "Navajo Chant" from *Dancing Gods* by Erna Fergusson, copyright © 1957 by The University of New Mexico Press. Used by permission.

Waterloo Music Company Limited for the words to "Land of the Silver Birch" from *Folk Songs of Canada* by Fowke-Johnston, copyright 1954. Used by permission.

Wonderland Music Company, Inc. for "Let's Go Fly a Kite" and "Scales and Arpeggios" by Richard M. and Robert B. Sherman. Used by permission.

Additional copyright acknowledgments and photo credits appear with the materials used.

Music autography by Maxwell Weaner
Cover art by Norman Laliberté

Contents

LET'S EXPLORE MUSIC

You are a musician when you . . . .

PERFORM

COMPOSE

LISTEN

Explore your book.
How many different ways will you **perform** music?
How many different ways will you **compose** music?
How many different ways will you **conduct** music?
How many different ways will you **listen** to music?
Explore your music book to find the many ways you, the musician,
   will **perform, compose, conduct,** and **listen** to music.

We're All Together Again

British Scout Song

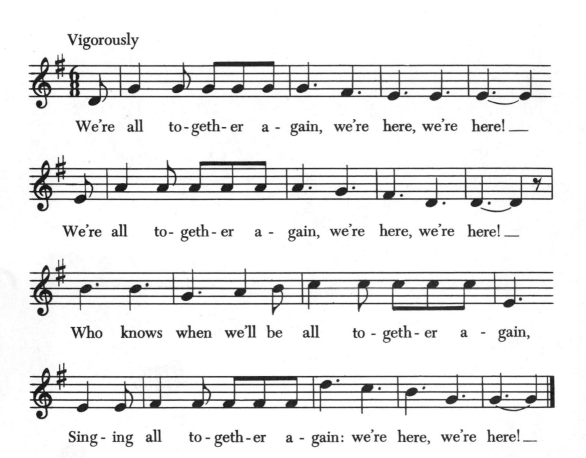

Vigorously

We're all to-geth-er a-gain, we're here, we're here! __

We're all to-geth-er a-gain, we're here, we're here! __

Who knows when we'll be all to-geth-er a-gain,

Sing-ing all to-geth-er a-gain: we're here, we're here! __

A Listening Adventure

You can have a listening adventure

- in your home
- in the country
- on city streets
- in your classroom

1 Say hello to four friends. Decide whether they answer with **high** or **low** sounds.

2 Slide on something. What kind of a sound did you make?

8 Listen to feet moving **evenly**, **unevenly**.

3 Think about a sound that is farther away than all others.

7 Place your ear close to something as it makes a sound.

4 Think about a sound that is coming toward you. What did you hear as it came close and passed by?

6 Make an echo.

5 Climb to a high place and describe a sound below. Sit under something and describe a sound above.

How many different sounds did you find?
Share your adventure with your classmates.

Tell Us Gentlemen

French Folk Song

1. Tell us gen - tle - men, Tell us all that you can do.
2. Tell us gen - tle - men, Tell us all that you can do.

Tell us gen - tle - men, can you play the big trom - bone?
Tell us gen - tle - men, can you play the tim - pa - ni?

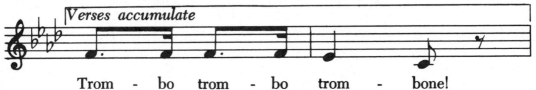

Verses accumulate

Trom - bo trom - bo trom - bone!
Tim - po tim - po tim - po!

Tell us, oh, can you play the big trom - bone?
Tell us, oh, can you play the tim - pa - ni?

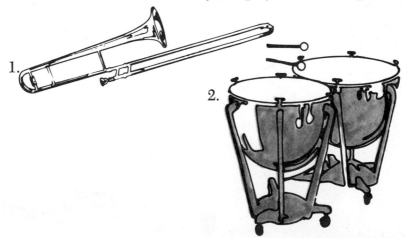

1.

2.

3. Tell us gentlemen. . . . .
   Can you play the trumpet?
   Trump - o, trump-o, trump-o.

4. Tell us gentlemen. . . . .
   Can you play the violin?
   Vi-o, vi-o, vi-o.

5. Tell us gentlemen. . . . .
   Can you play the clarinet?
   Clar-i, clar-i, net-o.

6. Tell us gentlemen. . . . .
   Can you play the silver flute?
   Flut-o, flut-o, flut-o.

What differences did you notice as each instrument was heard?

LOUD SOFT

Could you shout from a mountain........and hear an echo?

HELLO HELLO HELLO HELLO HELLO

How is the echo different from your voice?
Sing:

Hel - lo!

Ask five of your friends to be your echoes. Will they all echo at the
same time? How will their echoes be different from your "hello"?

If you pushed a big rock down a steep hill, how would it sound
as it fell?

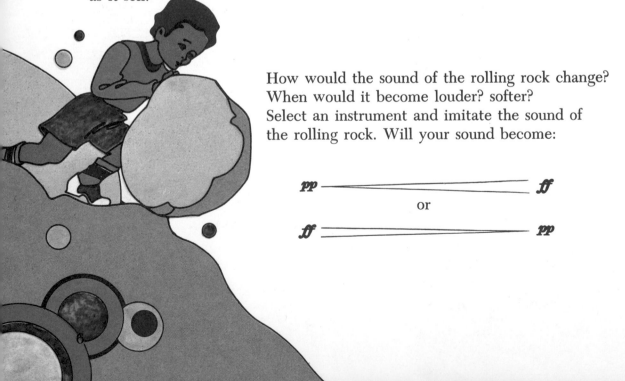

How would the sound of the rolling rock change?
When would it become louder? softer?
Select an instrument and imitate the sound of
the rolling rock. Will your sound become:

pp ————————————— ff

or

ff ————————————— pp

Deaf Woman's Courtship

American Folk Song

This music symbol means loud: **𝆑**

This music symbol means soft: **𝆏**

Can you find these musical symbols in this song?

Sing the song and follow the symbols.

With humor

1. Old wom-an, old wom-an, Are you fond of card - ing?
2. Old wom-an, old wom-an, Are you fond of spin - ning?

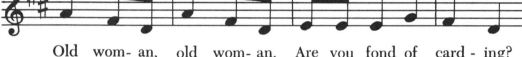

Old wom-an, old wom-an, Are you fond of card - ing?
Old wom-an, old wom-an, Are you fond of spin - ning?

Speak a lit - tle loud - er, sir! I'm ver - y hard of hear- ing.
Speak a lit - tle loud - er, sir! I'm ver - y hard of hear - ing.

3. **𝆑** Old woman, old woman, Will you darn my stocking? (2 *times*)
   𝆏 Speak a little louder, sir! I'm very hard of hearing.
4. **𝆑** Old woman, old woman, Will you let me court you? (2 *times*)
   𝆏 Speak a little louder, sir! I just begin to hear you.
5. **𝆏** Old woman, old woman, Don't you want to marry me? (2 *times*)
   𝆑 Oh, my goodness gracious me! I think that now I hear you!

How does change in **volume** add to the fun of the song?

The Noble Duke of York

American Folk Song

Introduction

VOICES

Rum, rum, rum pum pum.

p ——————————————————— *mf*

1. The no - ble Duke of York,
2. And when they were up they were up,

He had ten thou - sand men;
And when they were down they were down,

He marched them up to the top of the hill,
And when they were caught in be - tween,

Then marched them down a - gain.
They were neith - er up nor down.

CODA

VOICES

Rum, rum, rum pum pum.

mf ——————————————————— *p*

8

Wondering

Bohemian Folk Song

1. Where are the clouds that were here last night?
2. How far a - way is the dis - tant sky?

Why does the moon give a sil - very light?
How do we know which is you or I?

Who can tell? Who can say?
Who can tell? Who can say?

When will to - mor - row be yes - ter - day?
How man - y miles would be far a - way?

Find these musical symbols in the song.

p = soft mf = medium loud

p ——————— mf ——————— p

growing louder, growing softer

Use them as you sing.
Do they help you better express the song?

Many Sounds of Rhythm

What do you hear that . . . .

makes a steady beat?

makes a long, continuous sound?

stops and starts many times —
and has more than one sound?

has many sounds? Does each sound have a different rhythm
pattern?

Find instruments to suggest the sounds of rhythm you have
heard. Make up a rhythm composition.

- What sounds will you choose?
- How will you organize the piece?
- Who will be the performers?
- Who will be the conductor?

Symphony of Machines

Steel Foundry

Alexander Mossolov

Listen to the recording.
This music represents a composer's idea of how a machine sounds.
Do you think this is a big or little machine?
Listen again. This time make a sharp movement with your hand,
your arm, or your leg when you hear the heavy **accents**.

Who can be the parts of the machine?
Choose a partner and make up different movements for the parts
that you hear. You may begin the machine, and your partner may add
a movement to yours.

Make a machine using five people.
Begin by entering one part
at a time. Will you be pistons? levers?
chains? wheels? What else?

Look at the fresco on page 176.
Does it give you any ideas for
different movements?

11

Rhythm of the Beat

One, Two, Three

Collected by Venoris Cates

Can you hear the **rhythm of the beat?**
Clap the rhythm of the beat as you sing.

1. Head   and shoul-ders ba - by,   one!   two!   three!

Head   and shoul-ders ba - by,   one!   two!   three!

Head   and   shoul - ders,   head   and

shoul-ders, head and shoul-ders ba-by,   one!   two!   three!

2. Shoulders, knees
3. Knees and ankles
4. Ankles, knees
5. Knees and shoulders
6. Shoulders, head

Now use your hands and touch the parts of the body which are
mentioned in the words of the song.

Rhythm of the Pattern

Walk Together Children

Spiritual

Oh, walk to-geth-er child-ren don't you get ___ wear - y,

Walk to - geth - er child - ren don't you get wear - y.

Oh, walk to-geth- er child-ren don't you get ___ wear- y.

There's a great camp meet-ing in the prom-ised land.

Clap the long and short sounds of this **rhythm pattern**.

Find the words in the song that match this pattern.
Talk about the differences between the **rhythm of the beat** and
   the **rhythm of the pattern**.

Trip on a Train

by B. A.

Group 1

slow

Wher-cha go? Wher-cha go?

faster

Wha-cha do? Wha-cha do?

faster

Wha-cha see? Wha-cha see?

fast

Wha-cha git? Wha-cha git?

fast

Wha-cha hear? Wha-cha hear?

Group 2

Wich-i-ta, Wich-i-ta!

Went "Ka-choo!" Went "Ka-choo!"

Ditch - es, ditch - es.

Switch - es, switch - es.

Sh _____ Sh _____

Repeat the last line several times, becoming slower and

ff ——————————— *pp*

14

LINES OF MELODY

Draw lines to show how . . . .

     the basketball moves when you're dribbling

     the bowling ball rolls down the alley

     the softball moves when you're playing catch.

Make up three melodies that move the same way the balls moved. Use some of these bells.

Be sure you remember which bells you used. You might write down the letter names in order, or give each bell a number.

Can you think of another way to write down your melody?

Michael, Row the Boat Ashore

Spiritual

Close your eyes as you listen to this melody.
Can you draw its shape in the air?
Listen again and draw your picture on a sheet of paper.
Compare your picture with the note picture in your book.
Does your picture rise and fall the same way the notes do?

With feeling

1. Mi - chael, row the boat a - shore,
2. Mi - chael's boat's a mu - sic boat,

Hal - le - lu - jah!
Hal - le - lu - jah!

Mi - chael, row the boat a - shore,
Mi - chael's boat's a mu - sic boat,

Hal - le - lu - jah!
Hal - le - lu - jah!

3. Michael, row the boat ashore, Hallelujah! (*2 times*)
4. Sister, help to trim the sail, Hallelujah! (*2 times*)
5. Michael, row the boat ashore, Hallelujah! (*2 times*)

16

My Head and My Shoulders

Zulu Game Song

Here are four ways to show a picture of a melody. Try playing and singing each melody. Which picture was most helpful?

1.

chest
and
my
shoul - ders, my
mid - dle,
my
My   head   and

My   knees and   then   my   toes,   Oh,   my   knees and   then   my   toes,   Oh.

2.

1	1	1	3	5	5	5	8	7	6	5	5
My	head	and	my	shoul - ders,	my	chest	and	my	mid - dle,		

3	5	5	4	3	2	2	3	4	4	3	2	1	1
My	knees	and	then	my	toes,	Oh,	my	knees	and	then	my	toes,	Oh.

3.

C	C	C	E	G	G	G	C	B	A	G	G
My	head	and	my	shoul - ders,	my	chest	and	my	mid - dle,		

E	G	G	F	E	D	D	E	F	F	E	D	C	C
My	knees	and	then	my	toes,	Oh,	my	knees	and	then	my	toes,	Oh.

4.

My   head   and my shoul - ders, my chest and my   mid - dle,

My knees and then my toes, Oh, my knees and then my toes, Oh.

17

Awake and Sing

Old German Hymn
Words Translated by Catherine Winkworth

The first **pitch** of this melody is "1." Can you sing the first **phrase** with numbers? Can you sing phrase three with numbers?

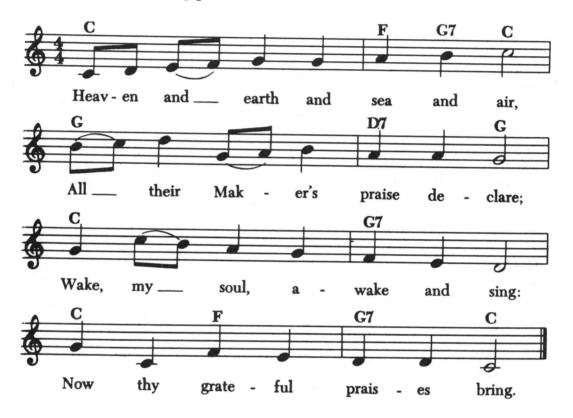

Heav - en and — earth and sea and air,

All — their Mak - er's praise de - clare;

Wake, my — soul, a - wake and sing:

Now thy grate - ful prais - es bring.

The first pitch of this melody is C. Can you play the first phrase on the bells? Use these bells.

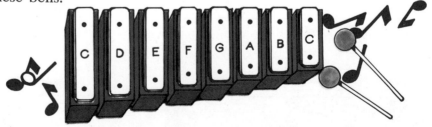

When you played the first phrase of this song, you also played a scale.

18

Sarasponda

Dutch Spinning Song

The first phrase of the melody on page 18 moves up by steps.
How does this melody begin?
What is the number of the first pitch in the song?
What is its letter name?
Look back at the song on page 18 to help you decide.

Sa - ra- spon- da, Sa - ra - spon- da, Sa - ra-spon-da, Ret - set- set!

Sa - ra - spon- da, Sa - ra -spon- da, Sa - ra - spon- da, Ret- set - set!

Ah - do - ray - oh!   Ah - do - ray- boom - day - oh!

Ah - do - ray-boom-day, Ret-set - set!   A - say- pa - say- oh!

The words of this spinning song have no meaning.
They suggest the sound of the spinning wheel as it turns.
Imitate the movement of the wheel as you sing.
Start slowly, then move faster and faster as you repeat
    the song several times.

Long John

Afro-American Folk Song

Listen to the recording. How does the music change each time it is repeated?

With his shi - ny blade, _ Got it in his hand, _

Gon - na chop out the live oaks That are in this land. _

He's Long John, _ He's long gone, _ he's gone, gone. ___

Like a tur - key in the corn, _ With his long clothes on. _

He's Long John, _ He's long gone, ___ he's gone.

Perform "Long John" in different ways.

one sound   two sounds   many sounds

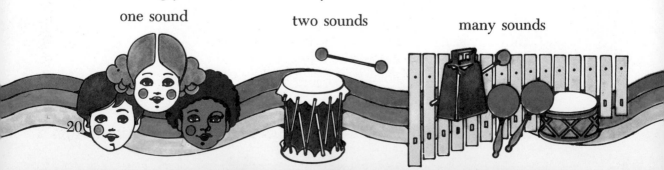

Play the Autoharp

Play one sound at a time on your autoharp.

Pluck a string.
Pluck another one.
Listen to different pitches.

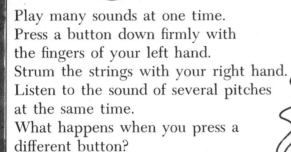

Play many sounds at one time.
Press a button down firmly with
the fingers of your left hand.
Strum the strings with your right hand.
Listen to the sound of several pitches
at the same time.
What happens when you press a
different button?

When you play the autoharp by strumming the strings, you are
playing a **chord.** Find these chords.

      Dm   F

Play these two chords over and over.

4
4   ♩   ♩ |♩   ♩ |

    F   Dm   F   Dm

Play while the class sings the first, second, and last phrases of "Long
John." Rest while they sing the third and fourth phrases.

Hitori de Sabishii

Alone and Sad

Japanese Folk Song

Hi - to - ri   de   sa - bi - shii,
1. By   my - self,   oh,   all   a - lone.
2. Let's   go   to - geth - er,   just   we   two.

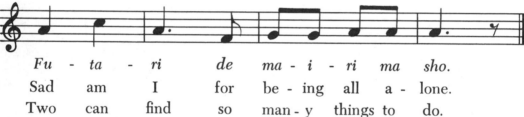

Fu - ta - ri   de   ma - i - ri   ma   sho.
Sad   am   I   for   be - ing   all   a - lone.
Two   can   find   so   man - y   things   to   do.

Add harmony to this song.

Soprano glockenspiel

Alto xylophone

Play these sounds together over and over in this ryhthm.

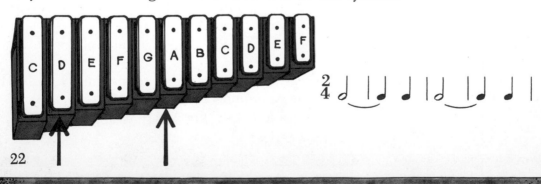

Take a Musical Trip*

Let's take a musical trip!
Put your finger on "GO."
When the music begins, slide your finger along the highway.
You should get to the first light at the end of the first phrase.
When the next phrase begins, continue your trip.

When the music begins a new melody, make your own highway
by drawing a line in the air.
How many stops will you make on these parts of your trip?

Each time the music repeats the first melody, follow
the musical map on this page.
What helped you know when you were coming
to a "musical stoplight"?

* SYMPHONY No. 24 in Bb Major,
Excerpt from "Andantino grazioso,"
by Wolfgang Amadeus Mozart

23

Down the River

American Play-Party Song

Listen to the music. Decide when it comes to a pause.
When music pauses, we know a **phrase** has ended.
How many phrases did you find? Did they all pause the same way?

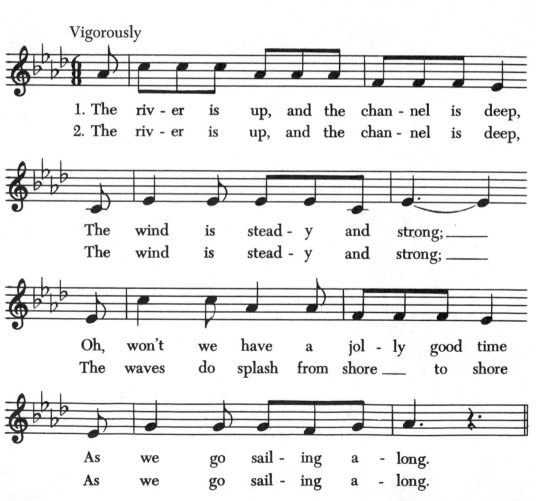

Vigorously

1. The riv - er is up, and the chan - nel is deep,
2. The riv - er is up, and the chan - nel is deep,

The wind is stead - y and strong; ____
The wind is stead - y and strong; ____

Oh, won't we have a jol - ly good time
The waves do splash from shore ____ to shore

As we go sail - ing a - long.
As we go sail - ing a - long.

Refrain

Down the riv - er, oh, down the riv - er, Oh,

down the riv - er we go - o - o!

Down the riv - er, oh, down the riv - er, Oh,

down the O - hi - o! _____

Look at the music. Can you find clues to help you know when
the music is going to pause?

A MUSICIAN KNOWS RHYTHM

Can you . . . .

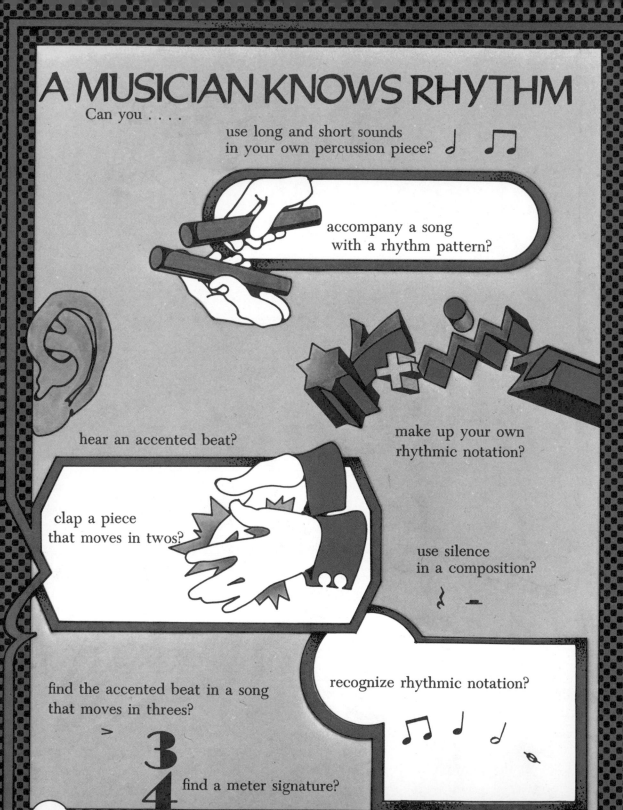

use long and short sounds
in your own percussion piece?

accompany a song
with a rhythm pattern?

make up your own
rhythmic notation?

hear an accented beat?

clap a piece
that moves in twos?

use silence
in a composition?

find the accented beat in a song
that moves in threes?

recognize rhythmic notation?

3
4
find a meter signature?

CHANGE AROUND

Rhythm moves in 2's

Step each beat and clap only on the beat marked: >

Change

Clap each beat and step only on the > beat.

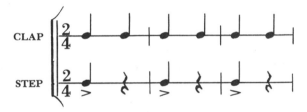

Rhythm moves in 3's

Step each beat and clap only on the accent: >

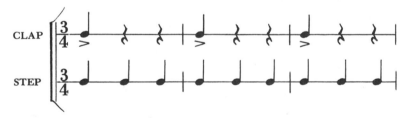

Change

Clap each beat and step only on the >

Let's Go Fly a Kite

Music by Richard M. Sherman
Words by Robert B. Sherman

Lively

Let's go fly a kite

Up to the high - est height!

Let's go fly a kite

And send it soar - ing

Up   through the   at - mos - phere,

Up   where the   air   is   clear.

Oh,   let's   go _____   fly   a

kite! _____

Which of these rhythms, when repeated, gives you the feeling
of a swaying kite?

Does this song move in threes or in twos? Why?

Sandy Land

American Singing Game
Words Adapted

Does this song move in twos or threes?
To help you decide, repeat the patterns on page 27 as
    you listen to the recording.
Which pattern fits the music?

1. Make my liv - ing in sand - y land,
2. Raise my ta - ters in sand - y land,
3. Keep on dig - ging in sand - y land,

Make my liv - ing in sand - y land,
Raise my ta - ters in sand - y land,
Keep on dig - ging in sand - y land,

Make my liv - ing in sand - y land,
Raise my ta - ters in sand - y land,
Keep on dig - ging in sand - y land,

La - dies, fare you well.

Plan an autoharp accompaniment.
The names of the chords you need to play are written above
the staff. Be sure to play on the accented beat.

Dance a Waltz

Evolutions (*Excerpt*)

by Henrik Badings

Is this a waltz?
Does it remind you of the
"Music Box Waltz" in any way?

Who might dance this music?
How would they move?

Music Box Waltz

by Dimitri Shostakovitch

How does a waltz move?

▬▬ ▬▬ — — — —
        or
▬▬ ▬▬ — ▬▬ — —
        or
▬▬ ▬▬ — ▬▬ — —

Make up a waltz step.
Take big steps on the **accents.**
Take short steps on the other beats.

Three to Get Ready
(*Excerpt*)
by Dave Brubeck

One for the money,
Two for the show
Three to get ready
And four to go!

Did the composer choose a good title
for his music? Why?

Tap the rhythm as you listen.

Get on Board

Spiritual

With strong accent

Get on board, lit - tle chil - dren, Get on

board, lit - tle chil - dren, Get on board, lit - tle

chil - dren, There's room for man - y a more.

The gos - pel train's a - com - ing, I hear it just at

hand; _____ I hear the car - wheels rum - bling and

roll - ing through the land. So

Canoe Song

American Indian Song

My pad - dle's keen and bright, Flash - ing with sil - ver.

Fol - low the wild goose flight, Dip, dip, and swing.

This song is made up of four rhythm patterns.
Look at the music. Find this pattern.

How is it like all the other patterns? How is it different?
Make it a melodic pattern by playing these two sounds.

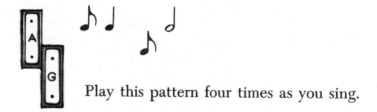

Play this pattern four times as you sing.

Corn Grinding Song

Navaho Indian Song

People use music in many ways. They sing as they work, as they dance, as they play. Listen to the Navaho Indian as she grinds the corn to make bread for her family.

33

Navaho Chant

Translation by
Dr. Washington Matthews

Play this pattern while the class chants.

Others may **improvise** accompaniments using different instruments for each line of the chant.

In beauty, I walk!

With beauty before me, I walk

With beauty behind me, I walk

With beauty below me, I walk

With beauty above me, I walk

With beauty all around me, I walk.

All instruments play together

In beauty it is finished

In beauty it is finished

In beauty it is finished

In beauty it is finished.

Land of the Silver Birch

Canadian Folk Song

1. Land of the sil - ver birch, home of the bea - ver,
2. Down in the for - est, deep in the low - lands,
3. High on a rock - y ledge, I'll build a wig - wam,

Where still the might - y moose wan - ders at will,
My heart cries out for thee, hills of the north.
Close by the wa - ter's edge, si - lent and still.

Refrain

Blue lake and rock - y shore, I will re - turn once more.

Boom de de boom boom, Boom de de boom boom,

Boom de de boom boom, Boom ___ boom boom. ___

Turn the Glasses Over

American Singing Game

Heartily

I've been to Haar - lem, I've been to Do - ver,

I've trav - eled this wide world all o - ver,

O - ver, o - ver, three times o - ver,

Drink what you have to drink and turn the glas - ses o - ver.

Sail - ing east, sail - ing west,

Sail - ing o - ver the o - cean,

Bet - ter watch out when the boat be - gins to rock,

Or you'll lose your girl in the o - cean.

Play a steady beat with sticks as you sing.

Can you find a pattern in the song which uses tones that move
with the beat?

quarter notes

Can you find a pattern which uses some tones that are **shorter
than the beat?**

eighth notes

Can you find a pattern which uses some tones that are **longer
than the beat?**

half notes

Tambur, Andandori

Hungarian Folk Dance Song

Tam - bur - am - bur, An - dan - do - ri,
Dance if it will give you plea - sure,
Best of all let's dance to - geth - er

Tam - bur, An - dan - do - ri.
What's the use of wait - ing?
By the fire - light blaz - ing.

Tam - bur - am - bur, An - dan - do - ri,
"Oh, my shoes a - part are com - ing."

Tam - bur - am - bur, An - dan - do - ri,
Don't you care, just hear the strum - ming.

Tam - bur, An - dan - do - ri.
You shall have some new ones.

Listen to "Tambur, Andandori" and to "Derry Ding Ding Dason."
Tap the beat of each song as you listen. Which song moves in twos?
Which in threes?

Look at the music for the two songs.
Can you find clues that would tell you how the beat moves
before you listen?

38

Sing each song and tap the beat as you sing.
Can you find a pattern where each tone moves
with the beat? Which note is used in that pattern?

♪ sixteenth note   ♪ eighth note   ♩ quarter note   ♩ half note

Derry Ding Ding Dason

English Round

Der-ry ding ding   da - son,   I   am John Ches - ton,

We   wee - don, we   wo - don, We   wee - don, we   wo - don,

Bim   boom,   bim   boom,   bim   boom,   bim   boom.

Did you find clues to help you know how the beat would move in
"Tambur, Andandori" and "Derry Ding Ding Dason"?

Did you find a **meter signature** made up of two numbers? Where?
Which number told how the beat would move?

Did you find notes grouped into measures by **bar lines?**
In which song did you find notes grouped in twos? in threes?

What is the number name of the beat note in each song? Can
you find it in the meter signature?

♪ 16   ♪ 8   ♩ 4   ♩ 2

39

A RHYTHM SCORE

Can you read a rhythm score?

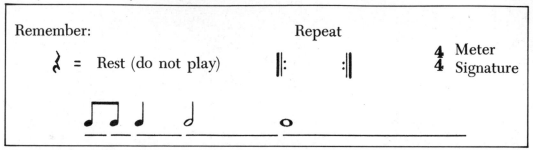

Remember:

𝄽 = Rest (do not play)

Repeat

𝄆 𝄇

4
4 Meter Signature

Can you decide how this music moves? What note sounds with the beat? Play each part alone. Play all parts at the same time.

When you have learned the rhythm score, play all the parts at the same time as an accompaniment for this poem.

Ping-Pong

by Eve Merriam

Chitchat	knickknack	crisscross	singsong
wigwag	gewgaw	flip-flop	mishmash
rickrack	riffraff	ding-dong	King Kong
zigzag	seesaw	tiptop	bong.

Way Down Yonder in the Brickyard

Written and Adapted by Bessie Jones

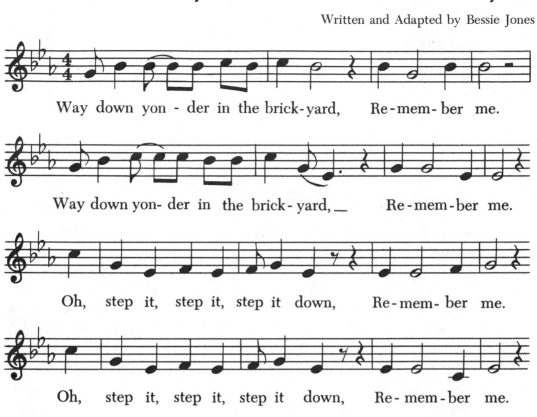

Way down yon - der in the brick-yard, Re-mem-ber me.

Way down yon- der in the brick- yard, ＿ Re -mem-ber me.

Oh, step it, step it, step it down, Re - mem- ber me.

Oh, step it, step it, step it down, Re - mem - ber me.

Oh, swing your love and turn a - round,

1. Re - mem - ber me. ＿ 2. Re - mem - ber me.

Tap and clap this beat:

CLAP

TAP

Can you continue this rhythm as you sing?

Written and Adapted by Bessie Jones. Collected and edited by Alan Lomax.
TRO — Copyright ' 1947 LUDLOW MUSIC, INC., New York, N.Y.
Used by permission.

Tongo

Polynesian Folk Song

Ton - go __ Ton - go __ Jim-nee bye __ bye __ oh

Jim - nee bye __ bye __ oh Ton - go __ Ton - go __

Oom ba de kim bye oh Oom ba de kim bye oh

Ooh - a - lay, Ooh - a - lay,

Mah - le - ka - ah lo way.

Mah - le - ka - ah lo way.

Play bamboo sticks in this pattern:

| tap floor | cross and tap together | tap floor | cross and tap together |

Play this pattern each time you sing the word "Tongo."

| Ton - (*floor*) | go, (*cross*) | Ton - (*floor*) | go (*cross*) |

Play this pattern for the rest of the song.

| Jim-nee (*bottom of stick*) | bye (*top of stick*) | bye (*bottom of stick*) | oh (*out*) |

43

Tinga Layo

Calypso Song from the
West Indies

Not too fast

Tin - ga Lay - o! Come, lit - tle don - key, come;

Tin - ga Lay - o! Come, lit - tle don - key, come.

1. My don - key walk, my don - key talk,
2. My don - key eat, my don - key sleep,

My don - key eat with a knife and fork.
My don - key kick with his two hind feet.

Tin - ga Lay - o! Come, lit - tle don - key, come;

Tin - ga Lay - o! Come, lit - tle don - key, come.

44

Listen to the recording and hear this interesting rhythm pattern.

How many times does it appear in the song?
Listen for interesting patterns in the accompaniment.
Perhaps you can play one of them on rhythm sticks or claves.
Claves are short, thick sticks. The people in the West Indies
often use them to accompany their songs.

A Poem

Haiku

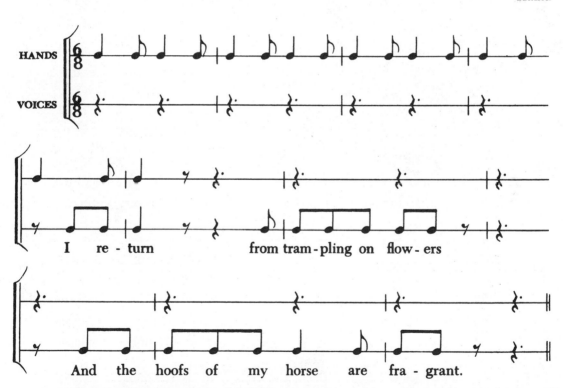

Does the sound of the hoofs continue throughout?
Perform the poem. Add this bell part as a special ending.

Hallowe'en

Music by John Wood
Words by Harry Behn

Mysteriously

1. To - night is the night when dead leaves fly
2. To - night is the night when leaves do sound
3. To - night is the night when pump - kins stare

Like witch - es on switch - es a - cross the sky,
Like gnomes in their homes far be - neath the ground,
Through brown sheaves and leaves al - most ev - ery - where,

When elf and sprite flit through the night,
When spooks and trolls creep out of holes
When ghoul and ghost and gob - lin host

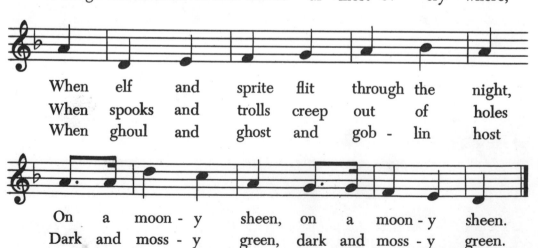

On a moon - y sheen, on a moon - y sheen.
Dark and moss - y green, dark and moss - y green.
Dance a - round their queen, for it's Hal - low - e'en!

This House Is Haunted

American Folk Song

This house is haunt - ed, this house is haunt - ed,

It fair - ly makes my blood run cold. _____

This house is haunt - ed, this house is haunt - ed,

It fair - ly makes my blood run cold.

𐄂 means "rest," do not sing.
How many times does this musical symbol appear in the song?

Plan an accompaniment for the song.
When the voice rests, make a scary sound with instruments, your
    voice, or other body sounds.

Will the music begin with singing or a scary sound?

The Banshee!

by B. A.

A banshee is a ghost,
She howls and wallows
As she mysteriously moves
Through the old dark hollow!

She comes in the night
And peers from room to room
Then returns at dawn
To the dark side of the moon.

Make up music to suggest the sounds of the banshee. Use an autoharp, a guitar, or the strings of the piano. Discover unusual sounds on your instrument by playing it in new ways. Use a plastic pick or a metal key and make scraping sounds. Tap the strings with a mallet. What other ways can you find?

When you have found interesting sounds, put them together as an accompaniment for the poem. Play your music as the class speaks the poem, or play it as a solo.

Banshee

by Henry Cowell

Henry Cowell was an American composer who explored new ways of making music. Listen to his music called "Banshee."

Can you decide what instrument he used? How do you think the performer makes the unusual sounds you hear?

Why do you think the composer's new sounds on a familiar instrument are good ways to express the banshee?

The Knight and Lady Delight

by B. A.

When does this chant move in threes? in twos?

Which verse should be **f** ?

Which verse should be **p** ?

CLAP

STAMP

1. Bright ar-mored Knight,   Bright ar-mored Knight!
2. La - dy De - light,   La - dy De - light!

Rode   a - way and joined the fight!
Cried for him all through the night!

49

The Gazelle

African Folk Song

Leader

Look what the ga-zelle does.
Gbo- di man- gi we - re.

Group

Look what the ga-zelle does, do it, oh!
Gbo- di man- gi we - re, Gbo- di o.

Leader

Now she rolls her ears.___
Gbo- di wo ti turn.___

Group

Now she rolls her ears, ___ do it, oh!
Gbo- di wo ti turn, ___ Gbo- di o.

Leader

Now she shakes her tail.
Gbo- di gu a gu.

50

Group

Now she shakes her tail, do it, oh!
Gbo - di gu a gu, Gbo - di o.

Leader

Now she lies down to sleep.
Gbo - di sun - gun sen - de.

Group

Now she lies down to sleep, do it, oh!
Gbo - di sun - gun sen - de, Gbo - di o.

Leader

Now she jumps up.
Gbo - di gua - ri.

Group

Now she jumps up, do it, oh!
Gbo - di gua - ri, Gbo - di o.

Follow the words of the song to help you think of an idea
for an African dance.

Play this part on a drum as you sing and dance.
Does the drum move in twos? in threes? both?

A MUSICIAN KNOWS MELODY

Can you . . . .

hear the rise and fall of a melody?

use high and low sounds in your own piece?

sing **steps** and **skips** of a melody using numbers? using letter names?

make up your own symbols to express a melody?

sing a **scale?**

find a melodic pattern in a piece?

play a melody?

hear a melodic phrase?

TRADE AROUND

Make up your own melody to match the feelings suggested by this poem.

Begin with these bells.
Use all of them for the first phrase.

Get up! Tis Day!
The sun is shining bright!

Trade some bells.
Use these for phrase two.

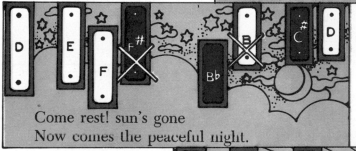

Come rest! sun's gone
Now comes the peaceful night.

Trade again!

Choose the set
you want to use.

But look! The sun
Returns once more at dawn.

And so repeats
The rhythm of its song.

Kenya Greeting Song

African Folk Song

The songs on this page and the next are from two different countries.
They use two different scales. One is **major.** The other is **minor.** Listen
to the two songs. Can you decide which song uses which scale?

Num - ber one, two, three, four, ___ five,

cha - lu - chi - le - li - la. Num - ber

li - la Bwa - na °(Ril - ey) i - mwe,

Cha - lu - chi - le - li - la. ___

Bwa - na°(Ril - ey) i - mwe, Cha - lu - chi - le - li - la.

°Insert name of person to be greeted.

Play the beginning of "Kenya Greeting Song" on these bells.

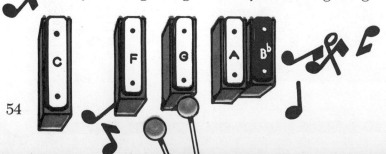

Play the beginning of "Tutu Maramba" on these bells.

Tutu Maramba

Brazilian Folk Song

Slowly

Tu - tú ___ Ma - ram - bá,   the   e - vil   spir - it   comes,

But   fa - ther   of   ba -   by pro - tects his   lit - tle   son.

Tu - tú ___ Ma - ram - bá,   the   e - vil   spir - it   comes,

Fine

But   fa - ther   of   ba -   by pro - tects   his   lit - tle   son.

Go   to   sleep   my   lit - tle   ba - by, sleep   and   do   not   fear;

D.C. al Fine

Fa- ther   al - ways watch - es   o'er   you,   love   is   al - ways   near.

55

AN EVENT

This is a melody clock.

Make your own melody clock.

Cut a circle from cardboard.

Write the letter names of these pitches around the edge.

Cut an arrow from cardboard.

Attach it to the clock with a brad.

Make a "clock scale" that uses six different pitches. To choose your six pitches, spin the arrow. Spin until you get six different letter names.

Find the bells with these letter names. Put them in order from low to high to make your clock scale.

Make up a "clock melody." You can go up or down from one bell to the next. You may skip back and forth among the bells.

Make a melody for this poem.

> Tick tock, tick tock,
> That's what most clocks say,
> But mine's a very special one,
> It sings the time of day!

How will you write down your melody to remember it?

56

Come Boating with Me

Italian Folk Song
Words by Lansing MacDowell

Here is the scale the melody of this song uses.
There are seven different letter names.
How many different pitches are there?

D E F♯ G A B C♯ D

With flowing movement

Come   boat - ing   with   me, _____

Come   boat - ing   with   me, _____

Un - der   the   stars 'mid   the   sound   of   gui - tars,

Come   boat - ing   with   me. _____

Scales and Arpeggios

Words and Music by
Richard M. Sherman
Robert B. Sherman

Listen to the recording as you look at the music.
Can you find patterns that move up by scale steps?
Can you decide what the word "arpeggio" means?

D   A7

If you're faith-ful to your dai - ly prac - tic - ing,

A7   D

You will find your prog-ress is en - cour - ag - ing.

D   G

Do me so me do me so me fa la so it goes,

D   A7   D

When you do your scales and your ar - peg - gi - os.

When the song begins, "1" is on "C," the very first note of the song.
Listen carefully. "1" changes when the singer starts to sing "Do mi so
do." Is the new "1" higher or lower than the first "1"?

Moto Perpetuo

from *Matinées Musicales*
by Benjamin Britten

Listen to this piece in which the orchestra has fun with scales.
The scales "move perpetually" up and sometimes down. The scale
is stated in the introduction. Then various sections of the
orchestra seem to show off as they play scale melodies.

Donkeys and Carrots

Belgian Round

In this song, "1" is "D," the first note in the song.
Can you learn to sing the song with numbers?

Don-keys love to munch on car-rots,

Car-rots don't love that at all!

Hee haw, Hee haw, Lis-ten to the sil-ly call.

Sing the song over and over.
Each time begin on a higher pitch.

then G

then F

then E

Begin on D

What happened? Was it always easy to sing?
Why do different songs use a different pitch as "1" or
home tone?

60

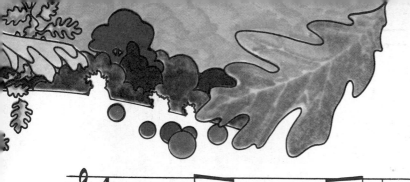

Harvest Song

Danish Song
Traditional Words

1. Out in the mead - ows the grain has been cra - dled,
2. Soon we shall har - vest the corn which is ri - pened;

Rye and wheat are stacked and soon the hay is in the barn.
Let us count our bless - ings as the grain is gath - ered in.

Trees have been shak - en and fruit has been gath - ered,
So in the full - ness of boun - ti - ful har - vest,

Home-ward now we wend our way up - on the fi - nal load.
Let us keep an o - pen heart for those who are in need.

Refrain

Glad - ness on ev - ery hand, Games and dance through-out the land;

Sing - ing mer - ri - ly we bind the hap - py har - vest wreath.

61

TIME FOR SCALES

Can you play the major scale
shown on this clock face?
Put all the bells in a long row.

Play only those bells that are circled
on the clock face.

The arrow points to the starting bell.

How many bells did you play?
What do you need to do to complete your scale?

Here is a picture of the C scale
   in notes.

C	D	E	F	G	A	B	C
1	2	3	4	5	6	7	?

Play the scale again as you watch the notes and sing the numbers.
What number do you think you should use for the last pitch? Why?

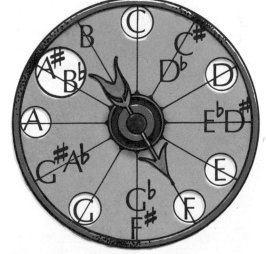

Play this major scale.
On which pitch will you begin?

Can you fill in the missing parts
   that describe the notes of
   the F major scale?

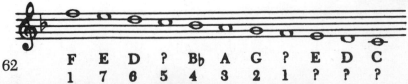

F	E	D	?	Bb	A	G	?	E	D	C
1	7	6	5	4	3	2	1	?	?	?

For Health and Strength

Traditional Round

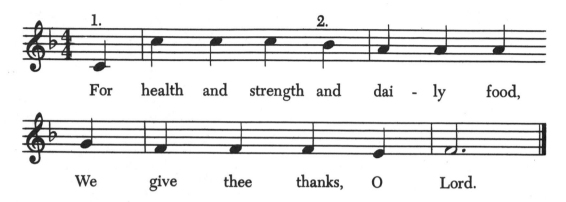

For health and strength and dai - ly food,

We give thee thanks, O Lord.

Which of these songs moves mostly by scale steps? Which uses arpeggios?

Play and sing each song.
Use the numbers for the F major scale, as shown on page 62.

Praise for Bread

Traditional Melody
Words by A. R. Ledoux

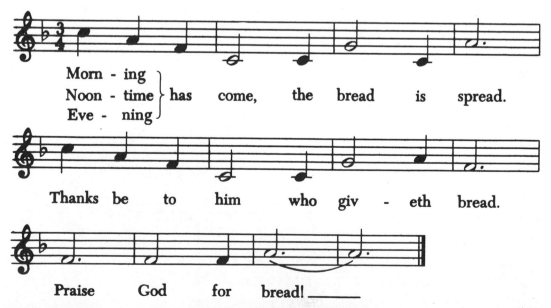

Morn - ing
Noon - time } has come, the bread is spread.
Eve - ning

Thanks be to him who giv - eth bread.

Praise God for bread! _____

America, the Beautiful

Music by Samuel A. Ward
Words by Katharine Lee Bates

Majestically

1. O beau - ti - ful for spa - cious skies,
2. O beau - ti - ful for pa - triot dream

For am - ber waves of grain,
That sees, be - yond the years,

For pur - ple moun - tain maj - es - ties
Thine al - a - bas - ter cit - ies gleam,

A - bove the fruit - ed plain!
Un - dimmed by hu - man tears!

A - mer - i - ca! A - mer - i - ca!

God shed his grace on thee,

And crown thy good with broth - er - hood

From sea to shin - ing sea!

Al Hasela

Hasidic Tune
Biblical Text

This work song is sung by the pioneers in Israel. "Al hasela" means "on the rocks." "Hah" means "hit." "V'yëtsu mayim ḥayim" means "fresh water gushes forth." Can you imagine what the pioneers are doing as they sing?

Al ha - se - la hah, hah, al ha - se - la

hah, hah, hah, Al ha - se - la hah, hah, v'

1.
2.

yë - tsu ma - yim ḥa - yim, ḥa - yim. ___

La la la la la la la la

la La la la la la hah, hah, hah,

la   la la la la hah, hah, hah, La   la

la   la   la   la   la   la   la   la   la   la   la.

Dance the Hora

Listen to the music. Then learn a circle dance that Jewish people enjoy on festive occasions.

The dance pattern is six beats long. Repeat the same pattern over and over until the music has ended. Begin with your left foot.

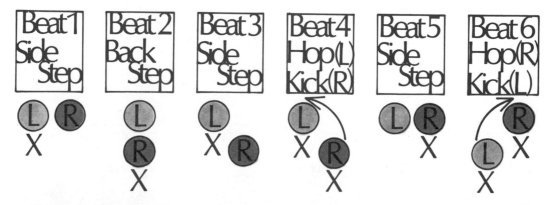

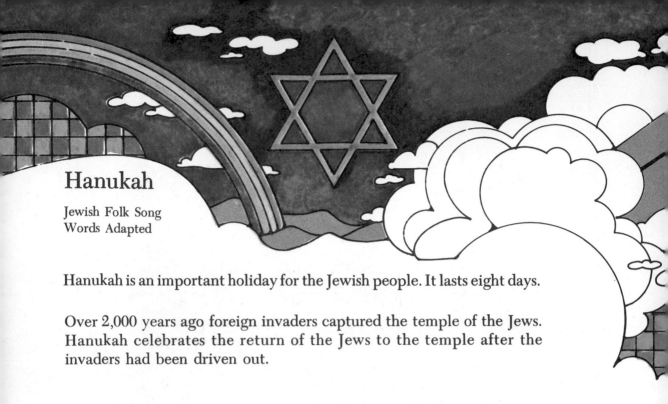

Hanukah

Jewish Folk Song
Words Adapted

Hanukah is an important holiday for the Jewish people. It lasts eight days.

Over 2,000 years ago foreign invaders captured the temple of the Jews. Hanukah celebrates the return of the Jews to the temple after the invaders had been driven out.

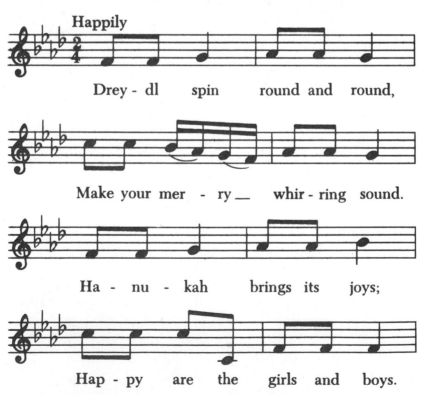

Happily

Drey - dl   spin   round and   round,

Make your mer - ry __ whir - ring sound.

Ha - nu - kah   brings its   joys;

Hap - py   are   the   girls and   boys.

The Frog and the Mouse

American Folk Song

1. There was a frog lived in a well,
2. He rode till he came to Mou - se's Hall,

Whip - see did - dle dee dan - dy O!

There was a mouse lived in a mill.
Where he most ten - der - ly did call,

Whip - see did - dle dee dan - dy O!

This frog he would a - woo - ing ride
"O Mis - tress Mouse, are you at home?

With sword and pis - tol by his side.
And if you are, oh, please come down."

With a har - um scar - um did - dle dum dar - um,

Whip - see did - dle dee dan - dy O!

3. "My Uncle Rat is not at home,"
   Whipsee diddle dee dandy O!
   "I dare not for my life come down."
   Whipsee diddle dee dandy O!
   Then Uncle Rat he soon comes home,
   "And who's been here since I've been gone?"
   With a harum scarum diddle dum darum,
   Whipsee diddle dee dandy O!

4. "Here's been a fine young gentleman,"
   Whipsee diddle dee dandy O!
   "Who swears he'll have me if he can."
   Whipsee diddle dee dandy O!
   Then Uncle Rat gave his consent
   And made a handsome settlement.
   With a harum scarum diddle dum darum,
   Whipsee diddle dee dandy O!

5. Four partridge pies with season made,
   Whipsee diddle dee dandy O!
   Two potted larks and marmalade,
   Whipsee diddle dee dandy O!
   Four woodcocks and a venison pie,
   I would that at that feast were I.
   With a harum scarum diddle dum darum,
   Whipsee diddle dee dandy O!

Suite No. 3 in D Major

Air

by Johann Sebastian Bach

Follow the rise and fall of the first important melody played by violins. This is a picture of the way it begins.

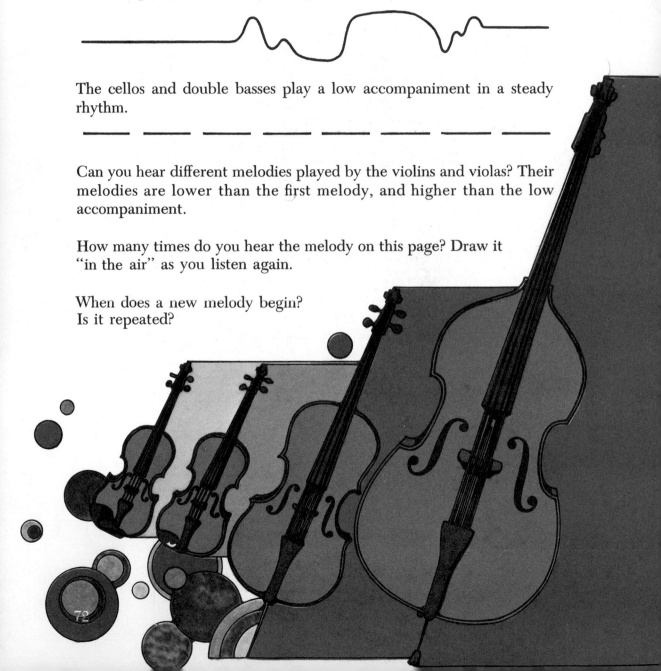

The cellos and double basses play a low accompaniment in a steady rhythm.

Can you hear different melodies played by the violins and violas? Their melodies are lower than the first melody, and higher than the low accompaniment.

How many times do you hear the melody on this page? Draw it "in the air" as you listen again.

When does a new melody begin?
Is it repeated?

Christmas Is Coming

Traditional English Round

Christ - mas is com - ing, the goose is get- ting fat!

Please to put a pen - ny in an old man's hat.

If you have - n't got a pen - ny, a ha'- pen- ny will do,

If you have - n't got a ha' - pen - ny, God bless you.

Can you plan a dance for this song? Perhaps you can use some
of these movements.

Join hands in a circle. Move to left or right.
Drop hands, walk to the center.
Walk backwards, to place.

What will you do on the words, "put a penny"?

Deck the Halls

Old Welsh Air
Traditional Words

In what ways do you and your family celebrate special holidays? This carol tells about ways people celebrated Christmas long ago. Yuletide is another word for Christmas. The Yule log was a huge log that was placed in the fireplace on Christmas Eve. It burned all through the twelve days of the holiday season.

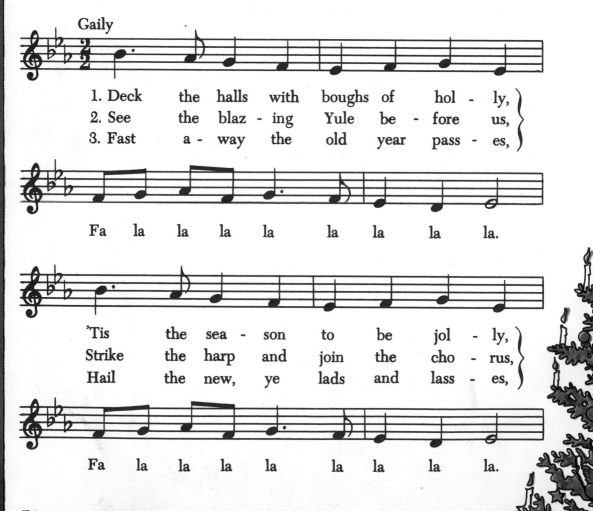

Gaily

1. Deck the halls with boughs of hol - ly,
2. See the blaz - ing Yule be - fore us,
3. Fast a - way the old year pass - es,

Fa la la la la la la la la.

'Tis the sea - son to be jol - ly,
Strike the harp and join the cho - rus,
Hail the new, ye lads and lass - es,

Fa la la la la la la la la.

Don   we   now   our   gay   ap - par - el,

Fol - low me   in   mer - ry mea - sure,

Sing   we joy - ous all   to - geth - er,

Fa   la   la   la   la   la   la   la.

Troll   the an - cient Yule - tide car - ol,

While   I   tell   of   Yule - tide trea - sure,

Heed - less of   the   wind and weath - er,

Fa   la   la   la   la   la   la   la.

Dance for Christmas

Dance as you sing "Deck the Halls."
Make up steps for each section of the music.

The A sections begin:

and end:

OR

The B section is:

How many times did you repeat
the A section? the B section?

O Little Town of Bethlehem

Music by Lewis H. Redner
Words by Phillips Brooks

Quietly

O lit - tle town of Beth - le - hem, How

still we — see thee lie. A - bove thy deep and

dream - less sleep, The si - lent — stars go by;

Yet in thy dark streets shin - eth The

ev - er - last - ing light; The hopes and fears of

all the years Are met in thee to - night.

'Twas in the Moon of Wintertime

Huron Indian Carol
Words by J. E. Middleton

Use this soft drum accompaniment as you sing:

1. 'Twas in the moon of win - ter - time
2. With - in a lodge of bro - ken bark
3. Ye chil - dren of the for - est free,

when all the birds had fled,
the ten - der Babe was found.
ye sons of Man - i - tou,

That might - y Git - chi Man - i - tou
A rag - ged robe of rab - bit skin
The Ho - ly Child of earth and heav'n

sent an - gel choirs in - stead.
en - wrapped His beau - ty round.
is born to - day for you.

Be - fore their light the stars grew dim,
And as the hunt - er braves drew nigh,
Come kneel be - fore the ra - diant Boy

and won - d'ring hunt - ers heard the hymn:_
the an - gel song rang loud and high:_
who brings you beau - ty, peace, and joy; _

Refrain

Je - sus, your King, is born; Je - sus is

born! *In ex - cel - sis glo - ri - a!*

Play a solo drum part before you sing each new verse. Continue playing
the beat, but slowly change the loudness and softness of your playing.

p ——————— *ff* ————— *p*

The Little Drummer Boy

Words and Music by
Katherine Davis, Henry Onorati
and Harry Simeone

Moderately

1. Come they told me pa - rum pum pum pum, ___
2. Lit - tle Ba - by pa - rum pum pum pum, ___
3. Mar - y nod - ded pa - rum pum pum pum, ___

A new born King to see, pa - rum pum pum pum, ___
I am a poor boy too, pa - rum pum pum pum, ___
The Ox and Lamb kept time, pa - rum pum pum pum, ___

Our fin - est gifts we bring pa - rum pum pum pum, ___
I have no gift to bring pa - rum pum pum pum, ___
I played my drum for him pa - rum pum pum pum, ___

To lay be - fore the King pa - rum pum pum pum,
That's fit to give our King pa - rum pum pum pum,
I played my best for him pa - rum pum pum pum,

rum pum pum pum, rum pum pum pum. _____
rum pum pum pum, rum pum pum pum. _____
rum pum pum pum, rum pum pum pum. _____

So to hon - or him pa-rum pum pum pum, _ when_ we come. _
Shall I play for you, pa-rum pum pum pum, _ on __ my drum?_
Then he smiled at me pa-rum pum pum pum, _ me and my drum. _

Can you be the drummer boy?
Play these patterns on the drum as you sing.

verse 1 and 2

$\frac{2}{2}$ 𝅗𝅥 𝅗𝅥 | 𝅗𝅥 𝅗𝅥 |

pum pum pum pum

verse 3

$\frac{2}{2}$ ♩ ♫ ♩ ♫ ♩ | ♩ ♫ ♩ ♫ |

pum rum pum pum rum pum pum rum pum pum rum pum

Can you find a special place to add this sound?

𝅗𝅥 𝅗𝅥

Poor Little Jesus

American Folk Song

1. It was poor _ lit-tle Je - sus,
2. { Poor _ lit-tle Je - sus, } Yes, yes, _
3. { Poor _ lit-tle Je - sus, }

He was born _ on _ Christ - mas,
{ Child _ of _ Mar - y, } Yes, yes, _
They _ took him from a man - ger,

And _ laid _ in a man - ger,
Did-n't have _ no _ cra - dle, } Yes, yes, _
They _ took him from his moth - er,

Was-n't that — a pit-y and a shame? Lord, — Lord, —

Was-n't that — a pit-y and a shame?

Can you add new verses of your own to help tell the story?
One verse might tell of the shepherds seeing the star.

Someone may play this pattern on the autoharp while others sing:

Dm Gm Dm

Six people might play the chords on bells.
Use these bells.

D minor chord

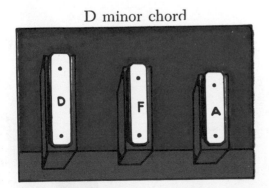

G minor chord

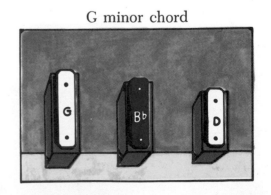

African Noel

Liberian Folk Song

Play this part as you sing the first two staffs of the music.

When does it become a harmony part? When is it a melody part?
Where could we use this part again in the song?

Sing No - el, sing No - el, No - el No - el. ___

Sing No - el, sing No - el, No - el No - el. ___

Sing we all No - el, sing we all No - el,

Sing we all No - el, sing we all No - el.

Sing No - el, sing No - el, No - el No - el. ___

Sing No - el, sing No - el, No - el No - el. ___

84

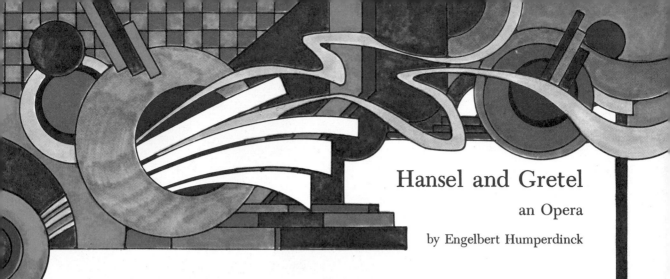

Hansel and Gretel

an Opera

by Engelbert Humperdinck

Do you know the story of Hansel and Gretel? Listen to parts of the story as told in an **opera**. Tell the other parts in your own words. When you see this sign, listen. ◆ When you see this, tell the story. ★

Act 1: Scene 1, in the cottage ◆

Gretel: Su - sy, lit - tle Su - sy, pray what is the news?
Hansel: Su - sy, lit - tle Su - sy, pray what's to be done?

The geese are run - ning bare- foot be - cause they've no shoes.
Who'll give me milk and su - gar, for bread I have none?

The cob - bler has leath - er and plen - ty to spare,
I'll go back to bed and I'll lie there all day,

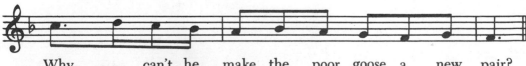

Why _____ can't he make the poor goose a new pair?
Where there's nought to eat, then there's noth - ing to pay.

85

Gretel: Broth-er come and dance with me, Both my hands I of-fer thee,

Right foot first, Left foot then, Round a-bout and back a-gain.

Act 1: Scene 3, father returns

Father:

The broom-stick, the broom-stick, why what is it for, why, what is it for?

Act 2: Scene 1, in the forest
Gretel:

1. There stands a lit - tle man in the wood a - lone,
2. His hair is all of gold, but his cheeks are red,

He wears a lit - tle man - tle of vel - vet brown,
He wears a lit - tle black cap u - pon his head,

Say who can the man there be, Stand - ing un - der - neath the tree,
Say who can the man there be, Stand - ing oh so si - lent - ly,

With the lit - tle man - tle of vel - vet brown?
With the lit - tle black _ cap u - pon his head?

Hansel and Gretel:

When at night I go to sleep, Four-teen an-gels watch do — keep, —

Act 3: The witch's house

Witch:

So hop, hop, hop, gal-lop, lop, lop! My broom-stick nag, come do not lag!

All:

See, O see the won-der wrought, How the witch her-self was caught,

The Overture

Listen to the opera's musical introduction called the **overture**. The composer introduces you to melodies you hear later in the opera. As you listen, point to the pictures that describe the parts of the opera the composer is using in the overture.

A MUSICIAN KNOWS HARMONY

Can you . . . .

combine tones
to make harmony?

hold a single tone while
others sing a melody?

echo what someone else sings?

hear two tones played at the
same time?

sing a different part
while others sing a melody?

sing one part and play another
part at the same time?

play chords on an instrument?

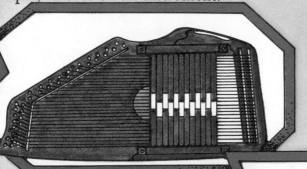

sing a round?

play an accompaniment for a song?

hear harmony sung by a chorus?

make up a piece that has harmony?

Explore Sounds of Harmony

You can make harmony on the piano by playing many tones at the same time. Experiment to find interesting combinations of tones.

 Find tones that are far apart.

Use three fingers on each hand. Spread them as wide as you can to find keys you can play at the same time. Listen to sounds that are far apart.

 Find tones that are close together.

Use three fingers on each hand. Find keys near to each other. Press down on all the keys at the same time. Listen to sounds that are close together.

Here is a composition for you to play.

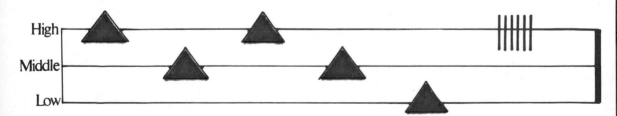

With these ideas, make up a composition that has harmony. Ask someone else to play it.

Can you make up a composition with harmony to play on other instruments?

Sing Different Parts

Who's That Yonder

Spiritual

Divide into two groups and sing this song.
Part 1 asks a question, part 2 answers.

PART 1 1. Who's that yon - der dressed in red?

PART 2 Must be the chil - dren that __ Mo - ses led! __

PART 1 Who's that yon - der dressed in white?

PART 2 Must be the chil - dren of the Is - rael - ite! __

2. Who's that yonder dressed in pink?
Must be Solomon tryin' to think!
Who's that yonder dressed in green?
Must be 'Zekiel in his flyin' machine!

3. Who's that yonder dressed in black?
Must be the hypocrites a-turning back!
Who's that yonder dressed in blue?
Must be the children that are comin' through!

Which part has only two different **pitches**?

92

The Goat

Traditional Folk Song

Sing this as a two-part song.
Group 1 sings the first melody pattern.
Group 2 echoes the pattern while group 1 holds the last tone.
Sing the entire song this way.

1. One day a goat ___ was feel-ing fine, ___
2. Sing a-di-os ___ but not good-bye, ___

Ate three red shirts ___ right off the line. ___
That goat was down ___ but not to die. ___

Jack took a stick, ___ gave him a whack, ___
He gave one yell ___ as though in pain, ___

And laid him on ___ the rail-road track. ___
Coughed up those shirts ___ and flagged the train. ___

Which rhythm pattern is repeated throughout this song?

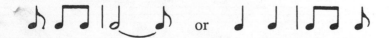

Trail to Mexico

American Folk Song

Look at the music. Listen to the recording.
Can you follow part 1 and part 2 on your page of music?

Now can you sing part 1?

and — change my way, _____

and change my way, —

To leave my na - - - - -

To leave my land —

tive land for a - while, _____

for just a - while, —

To trav - el west _____

_____ To trav - el west _____

for _____ man - y a mile. _____

_____ for man- y a mile.

Cattle

from *The Plow that Broke the Plains*
by Virgil Thomson

Cowboys often spend many lonely hours herding cattle. To pass the time, they sang songs about their horses, homes, and the cattle trail.

Can you hear three different cowboy melodies in this music? Different instruments take turns playing the three melodies.

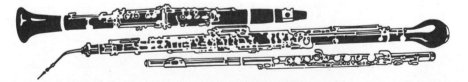

Other instruments play an accompaniment to add harmony. Sometimes the strings pluck an "um pah pah" pattern. Sometimes they play in arpeggios.

When the strings play the melodies, the full orchestra is the accompaniment.

A PROVERB

Setting by G. C. Nash

Early To Bed, Early To Rise,
Makes A Man Healthy, Wealthy, and Wise.

Speak this proverb using the parts below. Will everyone speak at the same time? Where do you see these musical symbols? 𝄾 𝄾

Accompaniment:

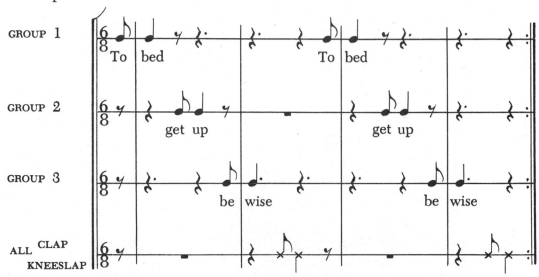

Proverb:

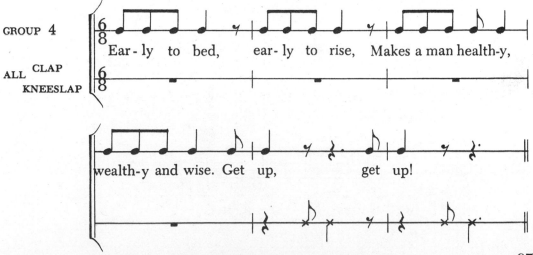

From *Rhythmic Speech Ensembles* by Grace C. Nash. Used by permission.

97

Cherry Bloom

Japanese Folk Song
Words Adapted

Gently

Cher - ry   bloom,   cher - ry   bloom,
Sa - ku - ra   Sa - ku - ra

Gent - ly   sway - ing   in   the — air,
Ya - yo - i   no   so - ra — wa

Sweet the   fra - grance ev - er - y - where,
Mi - wa - ta - su   ka - gi - ri

Pet - als   soft   and   col - ors — bright,
Ka - su - mi   ka   ku - mo — ka

Float - ing   clouds that   seem   to — say:
Ni - o - i   zo   i - zu - ru

98

Come and see, come and see,
I - za ya I - za ya

Come and see the cher - ry bloom.
Mi ___ ni ___ yu - ka - un

Notice the interesting sounds of the koto as you listen to the recording. Japanese folk songs are accompanied often by this ancient string instrument.

You can suggest the sound of the koto on the autoharp or violin. Pluck the F# and G strings in this rhythm.

F♯ G F♯ G

Listen to boys and girls from Japan sing the song you just learned. They belong to a choir called "The Little Singers of Tokyo." Can you find Tokyo on the world map?

Are You Sleeping?

Frère Jacques

French Folk Tune
Traditional Words

This song is a round. Listen to the recording.
Can you explain what a round is?

Learn to sing the melody very well.
Then divide into two groups and sing the song as a round.
Group 2 will begin when group 1 begins to sing "Brother John."

Are   you   sleep - ing,   are   you   sleep - ing,
Frè - re   Jac - ques,   Frè - re   Jac - ques,

Broth - er   John,   Broth - er   John?
Dor - mez - vous,   dor - mez - vous?

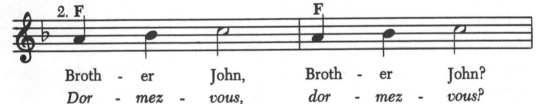

Morn - ing bells are ring - ing,   morn - ing bells are ring - ing,
Son - nez les ma - ti - nes,   son - nez les ma - ti - nes,

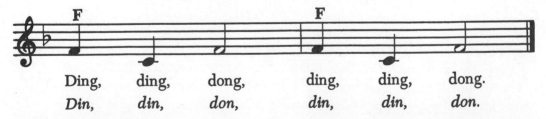

Ding,   ding,   dong,   ding,   ding,   dong.
Din,   din,   don,   din,   din,   don.

The Jungle

by B.A.

f The cat, —————— the cat, —————
He crouches, a tiger, so flat ———————
He SLIDES SLIDES
and slinks ~~~~~~~
In the jungle by the kitchen sink!

p The mouse, —————— the mouse, —————
Skiddles to a hole in the house. ~~~~~~~
He fearfully blinks, —————————
But is safe he thinks —————————
In the jungle by the kitchen sink!

Everyone could speak the poem together.

Someone might play this accompaniment on piano or bells:

Here is a part for a solo performer. Each time you see ——————— ,
make up a tune in rhythm with the poem. Use these sounds.

C   D   E   F#   G#   A#   C

101

Rich Man, Poor Man

American Nonsense Song

1. The rich man sleeps on a feath - er bed
2. The rich man goes in a car - riage fine;
3. The june bug has pret - ty gold - en wings,

With silk - en sheets of blue.
Big let - ters spell his name.
The light - ning bug the flame.

The poor man makes a pal - let
The poor man goes a - walk - ing
The bed - bug does not have wings

But sleeps the whole night through.
But gets there just the same.
But gets there just the same.

Add harmony with the bells. Listen to the bell accompaniment on the recording. Play it as someone sings. Use the B and C bells.

Add harmony by playing the autoharp. The names of the chords are shown above the staff. What is the difference between a chord and a melody?

102

Ah, Poor Bird

Old English Melody
Words Adapted

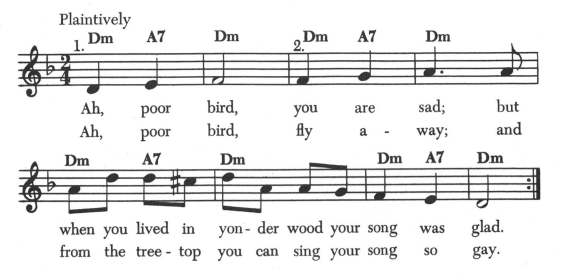

Ah, poor bird, you are sad; but
Ah, poor bird, fly a - way; and

when you lived in yon - der wood your song was glad.
from the tree - top you can sing your song so gay.

The Wise Old Owl

Traditional Round

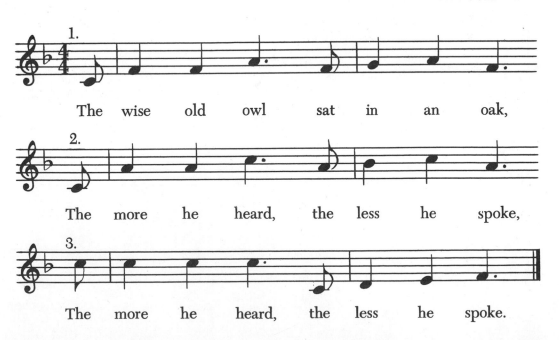

The wise old owl sat in an oak,

The more he heard, the less he spoke,

The more he heard, the less he spoke.

At the Gate of Heaven

Spanish-American Folk Song
Words Adapted

Follow the top staff of music and sing part 1.
Follow the lower staff of music and sing part 2.
Divide into two groups and sing both parts at the same time.
Which sections of this song are sung like a round?
When are you singing in harmony?

Part 1

1. At the gate of Heav'n ti - ny shoes they are giv - ing

Part 2

1. At the gate of Heav'n ti - ny shoes they are

To the lit - tle bare - foot - ed an - gels there liv - ing.

giv - ing To the lit - tle bare - foot - ed an - gels there

Refrain

Slum - ber, my lit - tle one,

liv - ing.   Slum - ber, my lit - tle one,

Slum - ber, my ni - ño, a - rru, a - rru.

Slum - ber my ni - ño, a - rru, a - rru.

A MUSICIAN KNOWS DESIGN

Can you . . . .

compose and conduct your own piece in ABA form?

hear when a musical idea begins, ends, repeats?

sing the verse of a song while others answer with the refrain?

make up a musical pattern, then perform it exactly the same way a second time?

dance a piece using a different movement for each section?

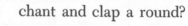

chant and clap a round?

make up symbols to show the design of a piece?

use A, B, or C to show the design of a piece?

WHOLE PARTS

Get ready!

New section

First section

Return to the first section

Same   Similar

Sections have smaller parts

Get from one section to the next

The ending   CODA

The Comedians

"March," "Galop," "Pantomime"

by Dmitri Kabalevsky

Listen to the "March." Can you find the parts that make up the whole? Can you follow this picture of the parts that make the design?

Can you find smaller parts that make up A?

Make your own picture for the design of "Galop" and "Pantomime." Which of the parts shown in the box will you need to use?

Add a Pattern

Se levanta la niña

Argentine Folk Song

Here is a short song. Make it a long song by adding a pattern each time you repeat the song. The Spanish words tell about a girl getting up in the early morning. Can you decide what time she gets up? It isn't always the same time!

Se le - van - ta __ la ni - ña a la u - na,

A la u - na de __ la ma - dru - ga - da;

*Verses accumulate**

Se le - van - ta a la u - na, La me - dio, la ze - ro, la na - da;

Ay, que lin - da __ la ma - dru - ga - da.

*Add an o'clock pattern each time you repeat the song.

2. Se levanta la niña a las dos,
   A las dos de la madrugada;
   Se levanta a las dos, a la una,
   La medio, la zero, la nada;
   Ay, que linda la madrugada.

3. Se levanta la niña a las tres, etc.

4. . . . cuatro, . . .

5. . . . cinco, . . .

6. . . . seis, . . .

Add a Phrase

There's a Little Wheel A-Turnin'

American Folk Song

1. There's a lit - tle wheel a - turn - in' in my heart, ___
2. There's a lit - tle song a - sing - in' in my heart, ___

There's a lit - tle wheel a - turn - in' in my heart,
There's a lit - tle song a - sing - in' in my heart,

In my heart, _____ in my heart, _____
In my heart, _____ in my heart, _____

There's a lit - tle wheel a - turn - in' in my heart.
There's a lit - tle song a - sing - in' in my heart.

Use these tones:

Make up one **phrase** to use as an **introduction.** Make up another to use as an **interlude** between verses. Make up a third **phrase** to use as a **coda.**

AN EVENT FOR 2, 3 OR MORE

Look at the designs on these two pages.
Make up a composition to match the first design.
Use bells or finger cymbals.

Make up a composition to match the design on page 111.
Use tambourine or drums.

Can you perform one of your compositions twice?
Borrow your neighbor's book and place it next to yours.
Cover the page you are not playing.

Use your two compositions to make a longer composition.
Arrange several books in order to show the form of your music.

Play your long composition.

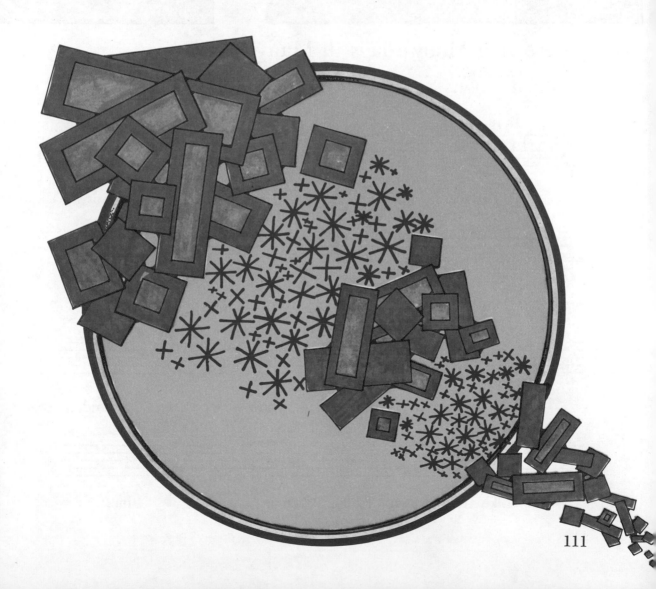

There Are Many Flags in Many Lands

Composer Unknown
Words by M. H. Howliston

In march time

There are man - y flags in man - y lands,

There are flags of ev - ery hue;

But there is no flag, how - ev - er grand,

Like our own Red, White, ⎯ and ⎯ Blue.

Then hur - rah for the flag, our coun - try's flag,

Its stripes and white stars, too;

For there is no flag in an - y land

Like our own Red, White,— and — Blue.

Someone may draw long curved lines on the chalkboard
as the class sings. Draw one for each phrase.

How many lines did you draw?
Were they all the same length?

Love Somebody

American Folk Song

1. Love some-bod-y, yes I do,
2. Love some-bod-y, can't guess who,

Love some-bod-y, yes I do,
Love some-bod-y, can't guess who,

Love some-bod-y, yes I do,
Love some-bod-y, can't guess who,

Love some-bod-y but I won't tell who.
Love some-bod-y but I won't tell who.

Refrain

Love some-bod-y, yes I do,

Love some-bod-y, yes I do,

Love some - bod - y, yes I do, And I

hope some - bod - y loves me too.

3. Love somebody's eyes of blue, *(3 times)*
   Love somebody but I won't tell who.
   Refrain

4. Love somebody's smile so true, *(3 times)*
   Love somebody but I won't tell who.
   Refrain

Can you find two large sections in this song?
What helps you know when a new section begins?

Valentine, Valentine

Words and Music by
Robert D. Sittig

Have you ever teased a friend? Sing this "teasing" Valentine song.
Boys and girls may take turns. Boys sing the first and third verses.
Girls sing the second and fourth verses.

Slowly

Boys: Val - en - tine, val - en - tine, who is my val - en - tine,
Girls: Val - en - tine, val - en - tine, who is my val - en - tine,

faster

Is it you? — Boys: 1. Mud tur - tle shells would be
Is it you? ____ Girls: 2. Foam rub - ber cake would be
3. Flow - ers and can - dy and
4. Gig - gles and whis - pers and

bet - ter than bells for my val - en - tine, yes,
eas - y to make for my val - en - tine, yes,
ev - ery - thing grand for my val - en - tine, yes,
may - be a kiss for my val - en - tine, yes,

Mud tur - tle shells would be fine. ____
Foam rub - ber cake would be fine. ____
I am your val - en - tine true. ____
I am your val - en - tine true. ____

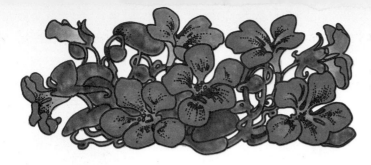

Hawaiian Rainbows

Hawaiian Folk Song

Something is missing from this musical picture. Listen to the recording. What should be on the empty staff? Describe the design of the song with letters.

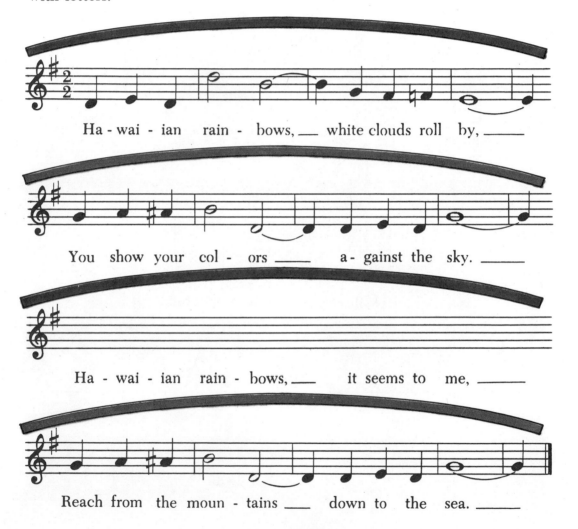

Ha - wai - ian rain - bows, ___ white clouds roll by, ___

You show your col - ors ___ a - gainst the sky. ___

Ha - wai - ian rain - bows, ___ it seems to me, ___

Reach from the moun - tains ___ down to the sea. ___

Plan movements to match each musical pattern.

117

Variations On A Theme

Symphony No. 94 ("Surprise")

Second Movement

by Joseph Haydn

This is a theme!   These are variations on a theme.

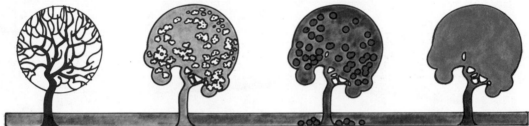

Listen to musical themes.

Can you hear their variations?

   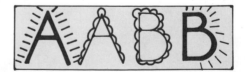

I Love the Mountains

Traditional

I love the moun-tains, I love the roll - ing hills,

I love the flow - ers, I love the daf - fo- dils;

I love the fire - side when all the lights are low.

Boom - dee - ah - da, Boom - dee - ah - da,

Boom - dee - ah - da, Boom - dee - ah - da.

Follow this picture of melody with your finger as you sing
the first phrase.

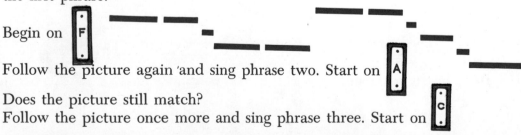

Begin on F

Follow the picture again 'and sing phrase two. Start on A

Does the picture still match?
Follow the picture once more and sing phrase three. Start on C

In what way are the three melodies alike? How are they different?

A RIMBLE IN RONDO

Do you know what a "rimble" is?
Move as you chant the rimble for the A section of this piece.

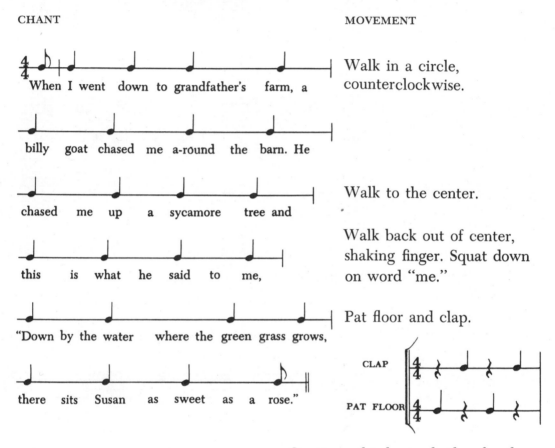

CHANT

When I went down to grandfather's farm, a

billy goat chased me a-round the barn. He

chased me up a sycamore tree and

this is what he said to me,

"Down by the water where the green grass grows,

there sits Susan as sweet as a rose."

MOVEMENT

Walk in a circle, counterclockwise.

Walk to the center.

Walk back out of center, shaking finger. Squat down on word "me."

Pat floor and clap.

CLAP

PAT FLOOR

Continue this basic rhythm for the B and C sections which follow.

Who can make up a rhythm pattern for the B Section?

Use these instruments and play as the class continues its rhythm pattern.

Who can make up a rhythm for the C Section? Use this instrument and play as the class continues its rhythm pattern.

Organize the sections into this form.

Can you decide what a rondo is? Play your "Rimble in Rondo."

The Moor's Revenge

Rondeau

by Henry Purcell

You have moved to a "Rimble in Rondo" which had three different sections organized like this.

Now, listen to a rondo. Is it organized in the same way? How many different melodies do you hear?

Can you dance as you listen to the music again? The A section is played by a string orchestra playing a majestic–sounding melody. What kind of movement does this suggest? The B and C sections each have different melodies. Will you use the same or a different movement for each of these parts?

What things in the music help you recognize each section of the music?

121

Joy to the World

Words and Music by Hoyt Axton

Moderate rock

Je - re - mi - ah was a bull - frog,

Was a good friend of mine.

Nev - er un - der - stood a sin - gle word he said, ___

But we al - ways had a might-y fine time. ___

Yes we al - ways had a might-y fine time.

Refrain

Sing-ing joy to the world. All __ the boys and girls __ now.

Joy to the fish-es in the deep blue sea, __

Joy to __ you and me. __

Can you use this music as part of a rondo?
Use the refrain as A.
Choose different songs for B and C.
Will any of the songs be repeated?
How often will you sing A?

A Musician Makes Music Expressively

Can you . . . .

express ideas with sounds that are:

f

mf

p

sing with sounds that are:

legato

staccato

play patterns in a tempo that:

choose tone qualities
to help express:

ritards

accelerates

How Do You Know?

When you see your friend, can you call him by his name?

When a friend telephones and doesn't tell you who he is,
  how do you know who is calling?

> Can you tell how someone feels
> by the sound of his voice?
> Say "Come here, right away" as though
> you were excited, sad, angry.
> What changes?

When you see an instrument, can you call it by its name?

> When you can hear an instrument
> but can't see it, how do you
> know what it is?

How would an instrument be played if it were to express the words
"come here, right away" in an excited way? a sad way? an angry way?

Choose a classroom instrument to express "Come here, right away"
in these different ways. What would you need to change when
expressing these different moods?

Night Herding Song

Cowboy Song

Imagine you are a cowboy. Sing "Night Herding Song" as you wearily watch over your dogies. Then pretend you are the cook on the trail calling the cowboys to breakfast.

Will you sing the songs on these two pages with the same tone quality?

Easily

1. Go   slow, lit - tle   do - gies, stop   mill - in'   a - round;
2. Lay   down, lit - tle   do - gies, and   when you've laid down

I'm   tired   of   your rov - in'   all   o - ver   the   ground.
Just   stretch your- selves out   for   there's plen - ty   of   ground.

There's grass where you're stand - in',   so   feed kind of   slow;
Stay   put,   lit - tle   do - gies,   for   I'm   aw - ful   tired;

You   don't have for - ev - er   to   be   on   the   go.
If   you   get   a - way   I   am   sure   to   be   fired.

126

Move slow, lit - tle do - gies, move slow, _____

Lay down, lit - tle do - gies, lay down, _____

Hi - o, hi - o, ___ hi - o. _____

Wake Up, Jacob

Cowboy Call

Freely

Wake up, Ja - cob, day's a - break - in', ___

Peas in the pot and the hoe - cake's bak - in'! ____

Ear - ly in the morn - ing, Al - most day, __

If you don't come soon, Gon - na throw it all a - way. _

(Hit on pan)

Wake up!

Originally titled "Cowboy's Gettin'-up Holler." Collected, adapted and arranged
by John A. Lomax & Alan Lomax. TRO — Copyright © 1938 and renewed ©
1966 LUDLOW MUSIC, INC., New York, N.Y. Used by permission.

127

SPECIAL SOUNDS OF GROUPS

Each instrument or voice has its own sound. The ways they are combined make many different sounds.

Look at the pictures on this page and the next as you listen to the music. Which group is performing each piece?

A Spanish Song for Recorders

Anonymous

If I Had a Hammer

American Folk Song

Hirtenlied (Song of the Shepherd)

by Franz Schubert

El colibrí (The Humming Bird)

by Gulio Sagreras

La grenadière (The Grenadier's Piece)

Anonymous

What the World Needs Now

Music by Burt Bacharach
Words by Hal David

129

Chebogah (Beetle)

Hungarian Folk Dance
Words Adapted

The design at the top of the page shows a picture of tempo. Listen to this song and the one on the next page. Follow the tempo design as you listen.

With spirit

In a cir-cle slide to left and don't be slow.
For-ward with a walk-ing step, then back in place.

To the right we slide a-gain as back we go.
Skip with el-bows joined and then your part-ner face.

Side-ward glide, side-ward glide, to the cen-ter glide;
Fast-er now, fast-er now, fast-er in and out;

Back a-gain, back a-gain, part-ners side by side.
Part-ners swing, part-ners swing, end-ing with a shout. *Hey!*

130

Four in a Boat

Appalachian Mountain Song

1. Four in a boat and the tide rolls high,
2. Choose your __ part - ner and stay all day,
3. Eight in a boat and it won't go round,

Four in a boat and the tide rolls high,
Choose your __ part - ner and stay all day,
Eight in a boat and it won't go round,

Four in a boat and the tide rolls high,
Choose your __ part - ner and stay all day,
Eight in a boat and it won't go round,

Wait - ing for a pret - ty one to come by'm by.
We __ don't __ care __ what the old folks say.
Swing __ that __ pret - ty one that you've just found.

"Chebogah" and "Four in a Boat" are both dances. The words help you know how to dance. They tell you when to change tempo as you dance.

Sound Shapes

Can you draw the shape of a sound?

Say each nonsense word.
How does it begin? end? What happens in the middle?

dit *whissch* **krabroomm** *piff* *Zelk*

Can you make the sound of a shape?

How will it begin? end? What will happen in the middle?

Were some of your sounds short and brisk?
These are **staccato** sounds.

Were some sounds smooth and sustained?
These are **legato** sounds.

Make up a rhythm pattern that uses some brisk sounds and some smooth
sounds. Ask someone else to play it. You can show them how to play
by using these marks under the notes.

staccato   *legato*

A Soldier's Tale

by Igor Stravinsky

Composers use different "sound shapes" to express musical ideas.
Listen to three parts of "A Soldier's Tale."
Can you imagine what is happening in the musical story?
Listen for **staccato** and **legato** sounds.
What else does the composer do to express his musical ideas?

The Siamese Cat Song

from *Lady and the Tramp*

Words and Music by Peggy Lee
and Sonny Burke

Listen to the recording. Do the singers sing with staccato or
legato sounds? Look at the music. What will help you know?

1. We are Si - a - mee - iz if you plee - iz,
2. We are Si - a - mese with ver - y dain - ty claws,

We are Si - a - mee - iz if you don't please.
Please ob - serv - ing paws con - tain - ing dain - ty claws.

We are for - mer res - i - dents of Si - am.
Now we look - in' o - ver our new do - mi - cile,

There is no fin - er cat than I am.
If we like we stay for may - be quite a - while.

3. Who is that who's living in that wire house?
   It must be a bird because it's not a mouse.
   If we sneakin' up upon it carefully,
   There will be some bird for you and some for me.

4. Do you seeing that thing swimmin' 'round and 'round?
   Maybe we could reaching in and make it drown.
   If we sneakin' up upon it carefully,
   There will be a head for you, a tail for me.

Plan an introduction and accompaniment for this song.
Which instruments will play staccato sounds?

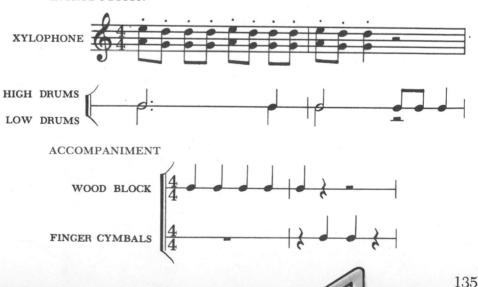

MAKING UP A 2-PART SONG

The Snake

by Karla Kuskin

Play this part on the bells as the class softly sings. Will you sing staccato or legato sounds? Look at the music. What will help you know?

Si - lent - ly   the   sil - ver snake goes,

Continue to play the bells and sing softly. Choose someone to make up a song using this poem and these sounds.

A snake slipped through
the thin green grass
A silver snake —
I watched it pass
It moved like a ribbon
Silent as snow
I think it smiled
As it passed my toe.

When the soloist and instruments stop, the class completes the song by singing:

Si - lent - ly   the   sil - ver snake goes,

In which part of this song were we singing harmony?
Which part had only a melody?

136

Clouds

Music by Arthur Frackenpohl
Words by Christina Rossetti

A performer can help express the composer's musical ideas.
How will you perform this song? Think about

tempo **tone quality** **volume** **legato** **staccato**

Wistfully

White sheep, white sheep, on a — blue — hill,

White sheep, white sheep, on a — blue — hill,

When the wind stops You all ___ stand still.

When the wind blows — You walk a - way slow.

White sheep, white sheep, Where do ___ you go? ___

Hawaiian Boat Song

Hawaiian Folk Song
Words Adapted

In my ca - noe I'm glid - ing, glid - ing;

My oars are flash - ing in the sun - light.

In my ca - noe I'm glid - ing, glid - ing;

The waves so gent - ly help me on.

Refrain

The u - ku - le - les, the u - ku - le - les,

My friends are strum - ming as we glide. __ glide.

Dance Musical Ideas

Listen again to the music from "The Comedians," page 107.
Choose one of the compositions and plan your own dance.
The composer expressed his ideas in sound.
Can you show his ideas in your movement?

melody

rhythm

harmony

changes in
instruments

slower — faster

legato

staccato

139

Raindrops

by Joseph and Nathan Segal

Play an introduction and accompaniment.
Begin with the sound of rain.

STICKS

ADD VOICE AND BELLS

Rain - drops,   rain - drops

ADD MORE VOICES

In   the   fall - ing   rain, ___

pp ———————————————————————————— *mf*

I   get to think- ing when it's ___ been rain - ing,

"Why ___ the   rain - drops?"

Guess I'm not think-ing like a flow - er's think-ing,

Guess I'm not feel- ing what a tree is feel - ing

In the rain - drops.

End the song by taking away

In the fall - ing rain,___

and

Rain - drops, rain - drops

and

STICKS

141

Childsong

Words and Music by
Neil Diamond

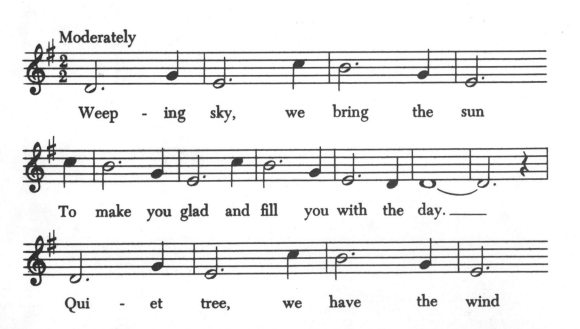

Weep - ing sky, we bring the sun
To make you glad and fill you with the day. ____
Qui - et tree, we have the wind

To make you dance and fill you with our play. ___

And you shall be glad ___ and you shall dance. ___

And you shall come to hear our song

And learn its tune be-fore it fades a - way. ___

A MUSICIAN EXPLORES MORE MUSIC

Look at the pictures.
What kind of music do they suggest?
What do you do when you hear each kind of music?

Look through the remaining pages of your book.
Find music that matches the pictures. Can you
perform or listen to this music?

Old Dan Tucker

American Folk Dance

Old Dan Tucker is back in town
A swinging everyone all around
First to the right:

and then to the left:

and then to the one that he swings best.

Get out the way, Old Dan Tucker,
Get out the way, Old Dan Tucker,
Get out the way, Old Dan Tucker,
You're too late to come to supper.

Listen to this old fiddler's tune. Can you make up a dance to go with it? Find a partner. Use hand clapping, foot tapping, and square dance swings. Can you sing as you dance?

My Farm

Mi chacra

Argentine Folk Song
English Words Adapted

el pollito

el patito

el chanchito

el gatito

el perrito

el burrito

Briskly

Come, let us see my farm, for it is beau - ti - ful,
Ven - gan a ver mi cha - cra que es her - mo - sa,

Come, let us see my farm, for it is beau - ti - ful.
Ven - gan a ver mi cha - cra que es her - mo - sa.

146

1. El po-lli-to goes like this:⎫ pi-pi ri,
1. El po-lli-to ha-ce a sí:⎭ pi-pi ri,

El po-lli-to goes like this:⎫ pi-pi ri.
El po-lli-to ha-ce a sí:⎭ pi-pi ri.

Oh, come now my friend, Oh, come now my friend, Oh,
O ven, ca-ma-ra-da, ven, ca-ma-ra-da,

come a-long with me, Oh, come now my friend, Oh,
ven, O ven, O ven, O ven, ca-ma-ra-da,

come now my friend, Oh, come a-long with me.
ven, ca-ma-ra-da, ven, O ven, O ven.

2. *El patito* goes like this: *cuac, cuac*

3. *El chanchito* goes like this: *joinc, joinc*

4. *El gatito* goes like this: *miau, miau*

5. *El perrito* goes like this: *guau, guau*

6. *El burrito* goes like this: *iji, iji*

147

Dance of the Comedians

from *The Bartered Bride*

by Bedrich Smetana

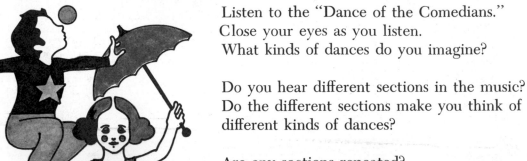

Listen to the "Dance of the Comedians."
Close your eyes as you listen.
What kinds of dances do you imagine?

Do you hear different sections in the music?
Do the different sections make you think of
different kinds of dances?

Are any sections repeated?
Do your imaginary dancers
repeat their dance steps?

Try dancing your own dance.
Your dance may follow the rhythm
or the melody of the music.

Divide into four groups; each group
may plan a different section.

Plan a grand finale for your dance.
Everyone repeat their dances for an exciting
ending to the music.

Sur le Pont d'Avignon

French Folk Song

Can you learn to sing this song by yourself?
Practice tapping the rhythm of the melody.
Sing the melody with numbers. The first pitch is "1."
Listen to the recording to learn the French words.
When you know the melody, someone may accompany the class
  on the autoharp. Play the chords shown above the staff.

Sur   le   Pont d'A - vi- gnon, L'on y   dan - se,   l'on y dan - se,

Sur   le   Pont   d'A - vi - gnon, L'on y   dan - se   tout en rond.

1. Les mes - sieurs font comm' ci,
2. Les bell's dam's font comm' ci, } Et puis en - cor' comm' ça.
3. Les sol - dats font comm' ci,

Listen to the song performed by French singers.
Does it sound the same as when you sang it?

The Tortilla Vender

Chilean Folk Song
English Words Adapted

The first time this song is sung, it is accompanied by the autoharp.
Can you hear when the chords on the autoharp change?

As I wan-der in the dark-ness,

With a lan-tern for my light. _____

I am sell-ing to-sta-í-tas,

I must sell them all to-night. ___

Refrain

Oh, _____ fresh tor-ti-llas! _____

Ah, _____ to-sta-í-tas! _____

150

¿Quien com - pra mis ___ to - sta - ti - tas? ___

Tor - ti - llas bue - nas?

One person may play chords on the autoharp to accompany the class as they sing.

Find the two chords you need: C and G7. Play in this rhythm:

$$\frac{3}{4}\ \downarrow.\ |\ \downarrow.\ |$$

Seven people may play chords on the bells. Another person may be the conductor. The conductor points to each group when it is time for it to play.

C chord

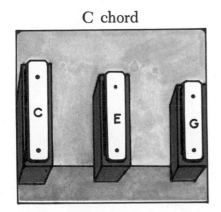

G7 chord

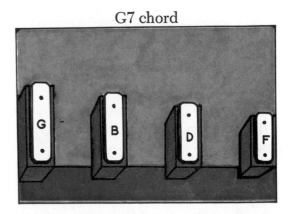

The performers tap their bells lightly over and over when the conductor points to them.

An Event For Two 2

Explore the sounds of the bells.
Find the lowest sounding bell . . . the highest.

Who can play this over and over again?

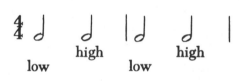

Call this Part 1 of the piece.

Use the bells that remain. Make up a melody for Part 2. Can you and your friend play Part 1 and Part 2 at the same time? Play your piece for the class. Can you give your piece a name?

QUESTIONS FOR THE LISTENERS

Did the performers find the lowest and highest sounds for Part 1?
Was the piece interesting?
Can you think of other ways to play this piece?

Row, Row, Row Your Boat

Traditional Round

Learn to sing this two-part round. The second group begins to sing when the first group sings "Gently down the stream." Listen to the harmony as you sing.

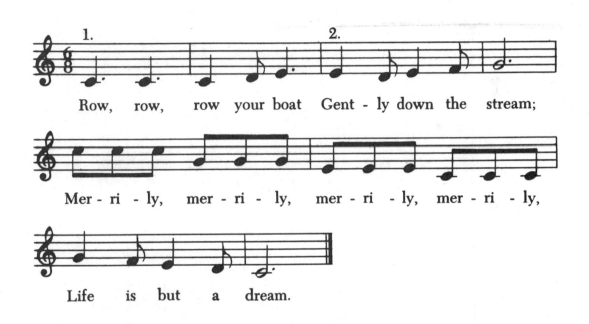

Row, row, row your boat Gent - ly down the stream;

Mer - ri - ly, mer - ri - ly, mer - ri - ly, mer - ri - ly,

Life is but a dream.

You can sing a round. Can you dance a round?
Plan different movements for each two measures.

Greeting Prelude

by Igor Stravinsky

Listen to the music.
Can you guess the name
of the melody? This
picture will help you.

Did you guess the melody? Did it sound "wrong"?
Listen again and look at this cake. Perhaps it
will help you decide what has happened to your melody.

The candles on the cake are "stretched out
of shape" and so was the melody! That is
because each tone of the melody is in an
unexpected place.

You can play "Hot Cross Buns" as a "stretched out" melody. First,
practice playing it on the piano. Use three keys.

3 2 1	3 2 1	
1 1 1 1	2 2 2 2	3 2 1

Three people may play together. Each person finds the same three
keys in different places on the piano.

Work together to play "Hot Cross Buns" as a stretched-out song.
Play only the pitches that are marked for your octave!

3	2	1	3	2	1
high	middle	low	middle	low	high

1111		2222	3	2	1
middle		high	low	middle	low

154

The Magic Garden

Words and Music
by Donald Jenni

Draw a curved line on the chalkboard as you sing each phrase.
Are all the lines the same length?
How do you know when each phrase ends?

Smoothly flowing

Swal - low, swal - low in the sky, may I

fol - low you as you fly to the

mag - ic gar - den? Swal - low, swal -

- low, not so high! You fly fast - er than

I can climb to the mag - ic gar - den.

Jig Along Home

Words and Music by
Woody Guthrie

Jauntily

1. I went to the dance and the an - i - mals come;

The jay - bird danced with horse - shoes on.

The grass - hop - per danced till he fell on the floor!

Jig a - long, jig a - long, jig a - long home.

Refrain

Jig jig - a jig jig - a jig a - long home,

Jig jig - a jig jig - a jig a - long home,

Jig a - long, jig a - long, jig a - long home,

Jig jig - a jig jig - a jig a - long home.

2. Fishing worm danced the fishing reel;
   Lobster danced on the peacock's tail.
   Baboon danced with the rising moon!
   Jig along, jig along, jig along home.
   Refrain

3. Mama rat took off her hat,
   Shook the house with the old tom cat.
   The alligator beat his tail on the drum!
   Jig along, jig along, jig along home.
   Refrain

4. The boards did rattle and the house did shake;
   The clouds did laugh and the earth did quake.
   New moon rattled some silver spoons!
   Jig along, jig along, jig along home.
   Refrain

5. The nails flew loose and the floors broke down;
   Everybody danced around and around.
   The house came down and the crowd went home!
   Jig along, jig along, jig along home.
   Refrain

The Star-Spangled Banner

Composer Unknown
Words by Francis Scott Key

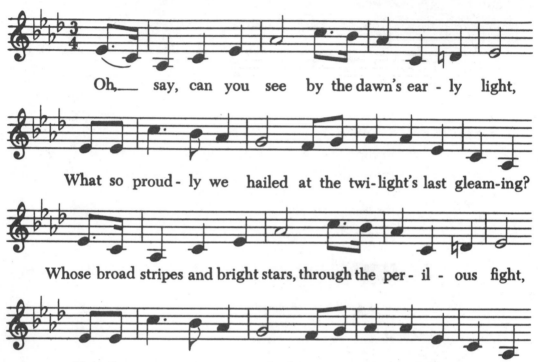

Oh,— say, can you see by the dawn's ear - ly light,

What so proud - ly we hailed at the twi-light's last gleam-ing?

Whose broad stripes and bright stars, through the per - il - ous fight,

O'er the ram-parts we watched were so gal- lant - ly stream-ing?

And the rock - ets' red glare, the bombs burst- ing in air,

Gave proof through the night that our flag was still there.

Oh, say, does that_ star-span-gled ban- ner_ yet_ wave_

O'er the land _ of the free and the home of the brave?

Vesper Hymn

Music Attributed to
Dmitri Bortniansky
Words by Thomas Moore

Use what you know about rhythm and melody as you learn the song.
Think about tempo, tone quality, and volume as you sing.

Experiment with these pitches on the bells and add harmony to your
song.

Let's Explore Art

Pair of Japanese screens.
Courtesy of the
Smithsonian Institution,
Freer Gallery of Art,
Washington, D.C.

Puppet Theatre by Paul Klee. Paul Klee Foundation, Museum of Fine
Arts, Berne, Switzerland. Permission S.P.A.D.E.M. 1970 by French
Reproduction Rights, Inc.

Let's Explore Art

The title of this section is "Let's Explore Art."
What will you explore? What is art?
You have music classes; music is an art.
Some of you go to dancing class; dance is an art.
You have art classes and learn to draw and paint; these are arts.
Why do we use the same word to describe things which are
so very different?

In this section of your book you will explore visual art.
You will see several types of visual art.
Discover the different materials artists use.
Discover different ways they use these materials in their works.
Find examples of art at home and in your community.
Create your own art.

The Starry Night, Vincent Van Gogh (1853-1890, Holland, France).
Oil on canvas.
Collection: The Museum of Modern Art, New York. Acquired through the Lillie
P. Bliss Bequest.

Circular Forms, 1912,
Robert Delaunay
(1885-1941, France).
Oil on canvas.
The Solomon R.
Guggenheim Museum
Collection, New York.

The pictures on these pages are painted with oil paints.
Each artist chose a different subject.
Talk about the subjects.
Talk about the ways the artists have used colors, shapes, and lines.

Still Life with Three Puppies, 1888, Paul Gauguin (1848-1903, France, Peru, Tahiti). Oil on wood.
Collection: The Museum of Modern Art, New York.
Mrs. Simon Guggenheim Fund.

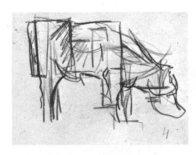

LEFT: *The Cow.* Three studies from a series of eight pencil drawings.
ABOVE RIGHT: *Composition* (The Cow). Gouache.
BELOW RIGHT: *Composition* (The Cow). Oil on canvas.
Theo van Doesburg (1883-1931, The Netherlands).
Collection: The Museum of Modern Art. Purchase.

Artists often practice before they complete their paintings.
Notice how this artist has changed his ideas as he worked.
The first picture looks very much like a cow you would see in a pasture.
Can you find the cow in the two completed pictures?

166

Self-portrait, 1655,
Rembrandt van Rijn (1606?-
1669, Holland).
Oil on canvas.
Courtesy, Kunsthistorisches
Museum, Vienna.

The paintings on this page
are self-portraits by two
famous artists.
Can you create a portrait
of yourself?

*Self-portrait with Seven
Fingers,* Marc Chagall
(1887-   , Russia,
France).
Stedelijk Museum,
Amsterdam.

167

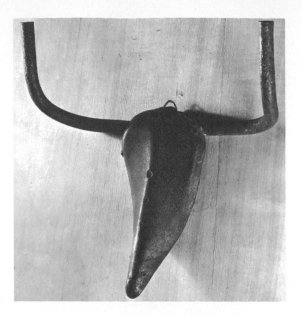

Head of a Bull by Picasso.
Collection of the artist.
Permission S.P.A.D.E.M. 1970
by French Reproduction
Rights, Inc.

Bearded Bull's Head, Sumerian
(2800-2600 B.C.). Copper.
City Art Museum of St. Louis.

The Flame, Robert Laurent
(1890-   , United States). Wood.
Collection: Whitney Museum of American
Art. Gift of Bartlett Arkell.

Indian on Horseback weather-vane. Wood and sheet iron. Abby Aldrich Rockefeller Folk Art Collection. Williamsburgh.

The examples of sculpture on these pages are from many different times and placcs. They are made from many different materials. Artists take the materials they find and form them into objects of art. Can you find interesting materials and form them into art objects?

Mischievous Cupid, 1755-1756, Étienne-Maurice Falconet (1716-1791, France). Marble. Rijksmuseum, Amsterdam.

Children on the Beach, 1940, Toni Hughes (1907-   , United States). Construction in plumber's hanger iron, galvanized wire cloth, screening, with various ornaments. Collection: The Museum of Modern Art, New York. Purchase.

The Liberty Bowl, Boston, 1768, Paul Revere (1735-1815, United States). Silver. Courtesy, Museum of Fine Arts, Boston. Purchased by Public Subscription and from the Francis Bartlett Fund.

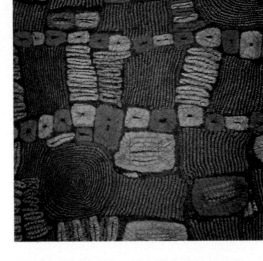

Raffia work with plangi and tritik decorative technique. Fragment. Baule (Ivory Coast). Museum Voor Land-en Volkenkunde, Rotterdam.

Rip Van Winkle, James Houston (1921-   , Canada), Engraved crystal. Courtesy, Steuben Glass.

Handcrafts were first developed to make useful articles in daily life. Many articles the craftsmen made are enjoyed also for their beauty. Artists use these crafts to create objects of art.

170

Corinthian black-figured crater from Cervetri, Rome, showing a married couple in a chariot with friends. Painted by the Three Maidens Painter, c. 560 B. C. Vatican Museum, Rome.

Bird Effigy Jar. Pottery with black painted decoration.
Socorro County, New Mexico.
Heye Foundation, Museum of the American Indian, New York.

Sugarbowl, c. 1825. Blown glass. Courtesy of the Brooklyn Museum, Dick S. Ramsay Fund.

White porcelain jug decorated with fish in 5 colored glazes. Ming, Emperor Chia Ching period (1522-1566).
Courtesy of the Fogg Art Museum, Harvard University: Bequest of Samuel C. Davis.

A Snow-covered Street by the Canal in the Shiba District of Edo, from
The Hundred Famous Views of Edo, 1857, Ando Hiroshige (1797-
1858, Japan). Wood-block print.
Victoria and Albert Museum, London.

This is an example of a print made from a wood-block.

People who design buildings are also artists.
Their creations are called architecture.

Greek Revival House, Ballston Spa,
New York. 19th Century.

Milo Stewart

Marina City, Chicago, Bertrand
Goldberg Associates, com-
pleted 1963. Concrete construction.

Lawrence L. Smith from
Photo Researchers

Musical Forms by Braque.
The Philadelphia Museum of
Art: The Louise and Walter
Arensberg Collection.

The Snail, 1953,
Henri Matisse
(1869-1954, France).
Gouache on
cut-and-pasted paper.
The Tate Gallery, London.
Permission S.P.A.D.E.M. 1974
by French Reproduction
Rights, Inc.

The artists combined different kinds of paper to create these works.

Kansas Land, 1968, Gordon Parks (1912-   , United States).
Photograph.

We have looked at different types of art—paintings, drawings,
sculpture, handcrafts, architecture, prints, photography.
Look again at the examples of each type.
Find other examples in your library, in a museum, or at home.

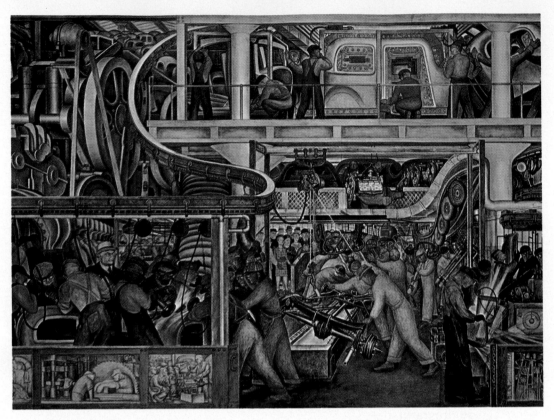

Body Presses and Assembly of Automobile Chassis (South Wall), Detail,
Diego Rivera (1886-1957, Mexico). Frescoes.
From the collection of The Detroit Institute of Arts. Gift of Edsel B. Ford.

Classified Index

Alphabetical Index of Music and Poetry